AN INCOMPATIBLE PASSION

a play in 3 acts

by
NIGEL PATTEN

«There is an incompatibility between love and creativity»
Percy Bysshe Shelley: Alastor (1815)

«A poet is a nightingale who sits in darkness and sings to cheer its own solitude.»
Percy Bysshe Shelley: A Defence of Poetry. (1821)

Strategic Book Publishing and Rights Co.

Copyright © 2013

All rights reserved—Nigel Patten

No part of this book may be reproduced or transmitted in any form or by any means, graphic, electronic, or mechanical, including photocopying, recording, taping, or by any information storage retrieval system, without the permission, in writing, from the publisher.

Strategic Book Publishing and Rights Co.
12620 FM 1960, Suite A4-507
Houston, TX 77065
www.sbpra.com

ISBN: 978-1-62516-425-4

Design: Dedicated Book Services (www.netdbs.com)

Cover photo (Shelley): Courtesy of the National Portrait Gallery, London.

Villa Magni (Shelley's last home): Courtesy of Eton College.

Acknowledgments

Any biographical study of a famous literary figure must of necessity rely largely on earlier research by other writers. From the very extensive material available I have drawn essentially from the following books: **Percy Bysshe Shelley** by James Bieri, **Being Shelley** by Ann Wroe, **Young Romantics** by Daisy Hay, **Mary Shelley** by Miranda Seymour, **Recollections of the Last Days of Shelley and Byron** by Edward John Trelawny and the journals and letters of Shelley, Mary and Claire Clairmont.

Author's Foreword

Sixty percent of the dialogue in my play is historically authentic, having been said (or written) by the character to whom it is attributed. On rare occasions I have deliberately given words to a different character than the one who in reality spoke them, or slightly modified the language to make it more accessible. I have also sometimes displaced time, using dialogue that was in fact spoken or written at an earlier date, and in one case modified an event without in any way diminishing its impact.

As this edition is for reading and not performance purposes, there are only stage directions where I feel they play an essential part in character development. In any case, no director should need the help of the author in staging a play and the reader can now allow his imagination to wander freely round the stage and people it with whatever action best suits his state of mind at the moment.

Prologue

In 1822 the Villa Magni, recently rented by Percy and Mary Shelley, stood on the rocky shore a mile or so from San Terenzo, a Tuscan hamlet across the bay from Lerici and overshadowed by a crumbling gray fortress. Centuries earlier it had been the site of a cult to Diana, goddess of the woods and the moon. Above it dark woods of chestnut and ilex cloaked the hills. Built directly on the rocks over four massive arches harboring cellars where local fishermen kept their boats and tackle, the ground floor was composed of a single vast living area, opening onto a wide terrace on the seaward side and overhanging the rocky tide line. Access to the first floor and its four bedrooms was by a single open staircase leading from the living area. The second floor provided cramped quarters for quarreling servants.

The scene is in darkness, except for a single spot downstage, revealing the figure of EDWARD TRELAWNY.

TRELAWNY

In the spring of 1822 Percy Bysshe Shelley, his second wife, Mary, author of **Frankenstein,** her half-sister Claire and another English couple they had known in Pisa, Edward and Jane Williams, rented a dilapidated villa on the rocky shore near Lerici, a fishing village on the Tuscany coast.

At the time Percy was thirty-two years old and Mary twenty-seven. From descriptive accounts by those, like me, acquainted with the poet, we learn that Shelley had a delicate, negligent even dishevelled appearance. His face was singularly engaging with a strongly marked intellectuality and a childish simplicity combined with great refinement. He had large bright blue rather wild eyes like a deer.

His eager vehement manner demanded the instant execution of any project that took his fancy. He overwhelmed all opposition. When awake he was fierce, energetic, and would argue instantly. He paced the room, gesticulating, like a dragonfly, dazzling in movement, and erratic in flight. He had a violent and excitable temper with sporadic outbursts of anger and rage. Then his gestures were abrupt, sometimes violent, occasionally even awkward. He could be terrifying when roused with his flashing eyes, wild hair and deathly white cheeks.

Physically he was rather odd, tall and slim to the point of limpness. His walk was willowy, low and stooping. When reading he leaned over his book, his eyes almost touching it. He often slid into a room, perched on a chair, talked and then disappeared as noiselessly as he came. He coughed violently at times and had pains in his side and chest, which he called 'spasms'. When they struck him, he fell on the ground, screamed, drummed his heels and pulled down cushions to cover him.

Guests noticed his odd starts, peculiar gestures and sudden fixed attitudes, as if frozen in abstraction. He often rubbed his hair fiercely so it was singularly unkempt and rough. Sometimes when visitors were announced he hid under the table or lay on the carpet like a dog or a faded flower.

His voice was, shrill, harsh and discordant. The intensity of feeling produced an electric effect. He was fond of wearing a long gray dressing gown, trailing at the heels. On more formal occasions he wore a large-brimmed leghorn hat, jacket and waistcoat and nankeen trousers, all fitting loosely to the body. He always left his shirt unbuttoned and washed his shock of curls by dousing his head in a bucket of cold water.

He believed his gastrointestinal symptoms were engendered by an earlier bout with syphilis. He feared it would degenerate into leprosy and condemn him to permanent ill health and a miserable death. He manifested an obvious persecution complex at times that verged on insanity. He suffered from anxiety symptoms, depressions, paranoid fears and terrible headaches, which he combated with doses of laudanum. He twice so overdosed himself that his life was threatened. The power of laudanum to soothe pain and give rest delighted him and retained a seductive hold on him all his life. He had periodic moments of panic when he lost consciousness.

He lived chiefly on tea, bread and butter, and occasionally drank lemonade made of a powder from a box, but his favorite dish was panada, water-soaked bread sprinkled with sugar and nutmeg.

ACT ONE

❖

MARCH 1822

SCENE ONE: MARY/JANE/ SHELLEY/CLAIRE/EDWARD

As the stage lights rise we find MARY SHELLEY seated alone on the settee. She is wearing a lilac chiffon shawl draped over her shoulders. At twenty-seven her hair is still a rich reddish gold, her complexion pale, her forehead high and intellectual. She had the reputation for an extreme and apparently unmitigated bad temper, no doubt the accumulative consequence of five miscarriages, the early deaths of two of their three children, for which she blamed her husband, and his frequent infidelities. The loss of her second child was devastating and marked the beginning of her depressive withdrawal from Shelley. She reacted to her son's death by turning inward, increasingly closing out her feelings for her husband.

MARY

Dear God! Eight years ago today! Shortly after four that momentous morning, Percy sent word that the chaise was waiting for us at the end of the street. Dressed in black silk gowns, we two young girls tiptoed down the stairs and out along the silent street to the corner of Hatton Garden. The strain and the first stages of pregnancy made me a poor traveler. We had to stop at every stage on the road to Dover, so that I could rest. Percy, convinced that we were being pursued, hired four horses at Dartford. The journey, nevertheless, took us almost twelve hours. We left Dover at dusk in a hired fisherman's boat manned by two sailors. Just before the sun rose next morning, a thunder squall struck our little boat. A heavy rolling sea swept in, almost capsizing us. Percy prepared himself to die, while Claire and I, mute with terror, pressed ourselves against his shaking knees. But the squall subsided and we even managed to sleep a little as the steady wind blew us towards the Calais shore. Here in Italy the scenery is very different. The hedges on the hillside behind the villa are myrtle. Their aromatic perfume weighs upon the sluggish noon air. The laborers repose under the olive trees, lulled by the sighing of the sea. In the evening they eat their meal under the open sky. The ground is alive with innumerable glow-worms, the air with fire-flies, humming crickets and heavy beetles. At dusk the west quickly loses its splendor, but in the fading beams sails the boat-like moon. Venus beams just above the crescent and the outline of the rugged Apennines dozes darkly below.

JANE WILLIAMS *enters discreetly from the upstage bedroom door. A year younger than Mary, Jane Cleveland was the sister of a general in the Madras army and, at sixteen, the wife of a bullying naval captain in the East India Company. She separated from him the following year, fell in love with Edward Williams, and proposed they elope. Like Mary, she broke with convention and left England as his wife, although no divorce had taken place. Jane is a slight, clinging young woman with dark hair, huge eyes, a swan-like neck and a long down-turned nose.*

JANE

There you are, my dear. Sitting all alone. Our little room upstairs is so full of packing cases still! I can not begin to imagine where we are going to put everything when it finally arrives.

MARY

Do you regret coming to us?

JANE

No, indeed. Our quarters in Pisa were most unsanitary and infested with rats. Maybe you regret offering us hospitality. You have been curiously silent since we arrived.

MARY

I have been thinking of my dead little boy again. This is foolish, I suppose, yet whenever I am left alone to my own thoughts and do not read to divert them, they always come back to the same point.

JANE

You still have a son. Such a charming lad.

MARY

A meager consolation for the two who are dead and the three never born. I sometimes wonder if their deaths be not some sort of expiation for sins committed in the name of youthful passion. How else can it be explained?

JANE

Does not the beauty of these surroundings in some measure constitute a consolation?

MARY

I hate this place. We see nobody and nobody sees us.

JANE

You hardly do the delightful setting justice.

MARY

I will admit that the evenings here are forever serene. We see a star in the east at sunset, Jupiter I think, almost as fine as Venus last summer. It only lacks a certain silver and aerial radiance. Unfortunately, we do not at present enjoy those brilliant skies that hailed us on our first visit to these shores. In November an almost perpetual rain confined us principally to the house. But when the summer sun does burst forth, it is with a splendor and heat unknown in England.

JANE

The heat this afternoon was almost oppressive as we strolled to the village. By good fortune Edward had remembered to bring my parasol. I think we glimpsed Shelley, still as a statue, seated on a bank of ferns above the shore.

MARY

Wherever the spirit of beauty dwells Shelley must be. The rustling of the trees is full of him, the waving of the tall grass, the moving shadows on the hills, the blue air that penetrates the ravines and rests upon the heights.

JANE

He does not feel the need of constant company, I am sure. Nature alone is adequate fellowship for a poet.

MARY

When we lived in Naples, we did not enter into society either, yet our time passed swiftly and delightfully. We read Italian and Latin during the heat of noon. When the sun declined, we walked in the garden looking at the rabbits and watching the motions of a myriad of lizards who inhabited the southern wall. There I felt as happy as a fledged bird. I hardly cared what twig I perched on to try my new-found wings.

CATERINA, the servant appears on the terrace, making frantic signs to Mary.

CATERINA

Il signor Shelley. Viene.

MARY

Well, of course he's coming. He lives here.

CATERINA

E nudo. Senza abito.

MARY

Good Lord. He has left his clothes behind again.

CATERINA just has time to block the top of the terrace steps as SHELLEY reaches the top behind her. He is returning from bathing naked. Water trickles down his nose. There is seaweed in his hair. He enters the room, screened by the servant.

MARY

Go and get some clothes on at once. Had you forgotten that we are no longer alone in the house?

SHELLEY sidles across the room like a crab behind the servant and stops beside JANE's chair.

SHELLEY

You see, I have to come though here to get upstairs. There's no other way. Only one staircase. The water was exceedingly cold today. The moon, poor fellow, is just rising. The trunks of the olive trees are already tinged with its silvery light.

MARY

Clothes, Shelley, clothes!

SHELLEY and the servant shuffle across the room to the staircase door.

MARY

Today Shelley is in a sad state of distress and excitement. His mind is astray. He is dreadfully nervous with the recurrence of the painful spasms that afflict him from time to time.

JANE

I remember that in Pisa he often complained of pains in his side.

MARY

Real or imaginary, his pains provide a convenient excuse for dosing himself with laudanum far beyond what is reasonable for his health. I hate this house and the country round it and am not well in mind or body either. My nerves are wound up to the utmost irritation. A sense of misfortune hangs over my spirits.

JANE

Have you no social contact with the neighboring village folk?

MARY

The locals here live in poverty beyond everything and speak a detestable dialect, quite impossible to comprehend.

SHELLEY returns now wearing a long gray robe like a dressing-gown, dragging round his ankles.

MARY

You can't wear that ghastly thing in company, Shelley. Go and change it.

SHELLEY

Certainly not. It is exceedingly comfortable.

MARY

Can you imagine? He used to wear it round the streets in Pisa. People laughed when he passed and call him 'Signora'.

SHELLEY

What the unmentionable townsfolk of Pisa think of my vestimentary attire is a matter of perfect indifference to me. It is comfortable and I like it.

JANE

Do you share Mary's unflattering opinion of the neighboring villagers?

SHELLEY

Of course, they are exceedingly simple, but they love to sing, dance and sport in the waves for hours, mostly half naked.

It is quite delightfully innocent. Mary hates the racket, but I love to join in.

He emits a wild burst of jarring high-pitched laughter and falls off his chair flat on his back.

MARY

Nonsense! Don't listen to him. He detests crowds. He takes refuge from society by delivering up his soul to poetry.

SHELLEY

Mary's right, as always. I shelter from the influence of human sympathies in the wildest regions of my fancy. Que toda la vida es sueño, y los sueños, sueños son. All life and being are but dreams.

CLAIRE

(appearing on the terrace, carrying Shelley's abandoned clothes.) And dreams themselves are but the dreams of other dreams.

CLAIRE CLAIRMONT is an attractive young woman, the same age as her half-sister. Since the initial elopement, she has lived with the Shelleys on and off. She conceived an illegitimate daughter, Allegra, with Byron during a visit to Geneva. Byron had arrived in Geneva in the spring of 1815. His wife had left him because of his incestuous relationship with his half-sister, Augusta Leigh. The Shelleys visited him daily at the Villa Diodati and Shelley went with him on a boat trip to the head of the lake. In May 1818 Byron leased the Palazzo Mocenigo on the Grand Canal in Venice. Claire sent him their daughter for Byron to raise. Despite Claire's protests, he put Allegra in a convent near Ravenna, where she died four years later. Byron was then living in Pisa, in the Casa

Lanfranchi, rented for him by Shelley. To be closer to Shelley, he then moved to Leghorn, where Shelley could visit him from nearby Lerici.

Rumors circulated that Claire also had a child with Shelley, Elena Adelaide, born in Naples, and falsely registered as being the child of Shelley and Mary. True to his theories of free love, Shelley was sexually intimate with both Mary and Claire. His feelings for Claire were overtly sexual and her musicality elicited erotic verses about her, which he hid from Mary. Mary in turn resented Shelley's confidences to Claire. Although perfectly aware of the pact of universal love that bound them, she always denied it in public. HARRIET WESTBROOK, Shelley's first wife, abandoned when he met Mary, refused to join the party in Italy and participate in a ménage à trois. She later killed herself by drowning in the Serpentine. The Lord Chief Justice confiscated the two children she had with Shelley and he never saw them again.

CLAIRE

You left your clothes on the rocks again, silly boy. Someone might have stolen them.

MARY leaps to her feet, darts across the room and seizes the bundle.

MARY

Give them to me! You had no business to remove them! I see you are determined to continue your improper behavior, despite my constant injunctions.

CLAIRE

Constant indeed. Heigh-ho, the Claire and Ma find something to fight about every day!

SHELLEY

Hush, Mary! Improper! That insidious word has never been echoed by these woods and rocks. Don't teach it them. It was one of the words my fellow serpent whispered in Eve's ear. When I hear it, I wish I were far away on some lone island with no other inhabitants than seals, sea birds and water rats. At Pisa Mary said a jacket was not proper, because others did not wear them. Here it is not proper to bathe, because everybody does. Oh, what shall we do?

He rummages behind a pile of books on the side table , drags out a sack of coins and tips them out on the rug.

SHELLEY

I brought these back from town last week and forgot where I had put them. Well, pick them up, Mary, and start counting. You know I am an infernal mathematician.

MARY

(on her knees)

Shelley can't be trusted with money and he won't have it.

EDWARD WILLIAMS has followed Claire into the room from the terrace. More intellectually limited than Shelley, Williams had left Eton for the navy after less than a year's schooling. He went on to serve with Shelley's cousin, Thomas Medwin in India and like him retired on half pay when the army was reformed after the Napoleonic wars.

EDWARD

I took the liberty of following Miss Clairmont back from the village, not being too certain of the way yet. There is quite a maze of tracks in the groves. That old castle across the bay has quite a sinister aspect. It encouraged me to hasten my pace.

SHELLEY

Sinister? Do you think so? Perhaps it shows its true beauty at evening only. We have much in common, that crumbling castle and I. *(He quotes Shakespeare)* "I too shall fall like a bright exhalation in the evening, and no man see me more."

MARY

Our modest ruin is hardly as forbidding as Chillon.

EDWARD

You visited it in the company of Lord Byron, I believe.

SHELLEY

I never saw a monument more terrible of that cold and inhuman tyranny which it has been the delight of man to exercise over man.

JANE

You were not tempted to rival Byron's epic with verses of your own?

SHELLEY

I never compete.

CLAIRE

We nearly lost the poor boy off the Savoy shore.

SHELLEY

It all happened a few cables off a miserable fishing village at the foot of the towering wooded mountains. The boat was heavily laden and the sea very high. There appeared some danger of swamping from the tremendous storm with waves at least fifteen feet high. We all prepared for a swamp as it was impossible to keep the smallest sail and the water began to break over the bow. One of the boatmen, a dreadfully stupid fellow, mishandled the manoeuvre and the boat was filling fast. Byron took off his coat. He made me do the same and take hold of an oar. Being an expert swimmer, he told me he could save me, if I did not struggle when he took hold of me, unless we got smashed against the sharp rocks with an awkward surf on them. We were then about a hundred yards from the shore and the boat in peril. I told him I had no notion of being saved. He would have enough to do to save himself. I felt in this near prospect of death a mixture of sensations, among which terror entered, though only subordinately. My feeling would have been less painful had I been alone. I knew that my companion would have attempted to save me and I was overcome with humiliation when I thought that his life might have been risked to preserve mine. Finally the storm cleared away leaving only finely-woven webs of vapor, flocks of fleecy slow-moving clouds which vanished before sunset.

EDWARD

Where were you, Miss Clairmont, during this alarming episode?

MARY

Oh, the ladies were confined to their apartments in Geneva on that occasion. We all visited Chillon some weeks later on our route to Chamonix.

CLAIRE

You need not include me in that "all". I seem to recollect that I was not invited.

MARY

It suited you well enough not to be invited. You could philander with Byron by the stimulating waters of the lake. And we know where that led to.

Claire's daughter Allegra (Alba) with Byron was conceived in Geneva while the Shelleys were away at Chamonix.

SHELLEY

(anxious to change the subject)

The immensity of the Alps staggers the imagination. They so far surpass all conception that it requires an effort of understanding to believe that they are indeed mountains. Mont Blanc and its connected mountains exceeded and rendered insignificant all we had before seen or imagined.

MARY

The snowy summits are often covered with cloud, their base furrowed with dreadful gaps. The immensity of those aerial summits excited in us both a sentiment of ecstatic wonder near to madness.

SHELLEY

The ravines, clothed with gigantic pines and black within their depth below, are so deep that the very roaring of the untameable river rolling through them can not be heard above. The cascading water falls in thick tawny folds. It flakes off like solid snow gliding down a mountain, like the folding of linen thrown carelessly down.

MARY

All was as much our own, as if we had been the creators of such impressions in the minds of others.

EDWARD

No doubt Miss Clairmont partook of other excursions, just as memorable.

CLAIRE

Indeed, I well remember another delightful lake in the German part of Switzerland on our first visit to that country. It was a deep and narrow water about nine miles in length and skirted on both sides with rocks uncommonly wild and romantic, some perpendicular, some stretching over our heads. They intercepted the view of the upper sky and were clothed for the most part in forests of beech and pine that extended down to the very edge of the water. The lake was as smooth as crystal. The arching precipices that enclosed it gave a peculiar solemnity to the gloom. I thought of William Tell and the glorious founders of Swiss liberty. I thought of the simple manners which still prevail in the primitive cantons. I felt as if I were in the wildest and most uninhabited islands of the South Seas.

MARY

Really, Claire! Your imagination has quite dominated your memory. The inhabitants of your primitive cantons are most immoderately stupid and almost ugly to deformity.

SHELLEY

Hush, Mary. You know what she is trying to say. Nature was the poet on that lakeside. Its harmony held our spirits more breathless than that of the divinest. One would think that the surrounding mountains formed a living being and that the frozen blood forever flowed through his stony veins.

EDWARD

On our passage through Geneva I came across Mr. Rousseau's *"Rêveries du promeneur solitaire."* His descriptions and feelings for nature are quite wonderful too.

SHELLEY

Naturally, a fellow admirer of Plutarch.

JANE

Did he not have five children with a hotel servant and send them all to a foundling hospital? Was that due to his admiration for Plutarch?

MARY

It is hardly surprising that they burnt his books in Geneva.

SHELLEY

Now, Mary, you know his books were burnt because his philosophical skepticism was offensive to the authorities, not because he sent his children to the hospice. He was convinced that modern society was rotten to the roots. It still is.

CLAIRE

But he believed that man is naturally good, did he not?

SHELLEY

No, he believed that the moral confusion in society was the consequence of his environment and its inequalities being unsuited to his nature.

CLAIRE

And what is his nature, Percy?

MARY

If you ask Shelley, who incidentally suffers from the same persecution mania – yes, you do – he will tell you that self-absorbed people like him demand that others should feel towards him in a way that he, though he does not know it, is incapable of feeling towards them.

CLAIRE

If I wrote a novel it would be about a young woman who dreams of love more than she has ever known it.

MARY

That is certainly not your case, is it?

JANE

Everybody longs to become emotionally independent of others and still feel a need for their affection.

EDWARD

I hope you are not suggesting that we are emotionally independent of each other, my dear. It might lead to confusion.

SHELLEY

We all crave secretly or not to go beyond ourselves. It is because we enter into the meditations, designs and destinies of that something beyond ourselves that the ocean, the glacier, the cataract, the tempest, the volcano have each a spirit. It animates us with a tingling joy. The singing of birds, the motion of leaves, the sensation of the odorous earth and the freshness of the living wind are sweet. And this is love. This is the religion of eternity.

CLAIRE

What is love, Percy?

SHELLEY

What is love? It is that powerful attraction towards all that we conceive or fear or hope beyond ourselves. It brings to mind what our mutual friend, Lord B, wrote about Rousseau: "His love was passion's essence, as a tree on fire by lightning, with ethereal flame kindled he was, and blasted."

CLAIRE

How blasted?

MARY

His passion led to the loss of his mind, Claire. Beware of passion. Our beloved Shelley has always been haunted with a passion too. He pines after the wildest and most extravagant romances, stories of haunted castles, bandits, murderers or featuring perverse, incestuous priests.

SHELLEY

My need to live in a fantasy world has always been far greater than that of most men. Only once I strove to be a successful apostle of the sole true religion – the religion of philanthropy.

EDWARD

Did you not try to improve the plight of the poor in Ireland?

SHELLEY

With Harriet I crossed the Irish Sea bearing the olive branch of hope. I harangued the poor in the streets of Dublin. I enjoined them to throw off the chains of ignominious slavery and revolt against the tyranny of social injustice.

EDWARD

May we know if you were successful?

SHELLEY

Most men, I soon became convinced, live in a state of squalid ignorance and moral imbecility. I discovered that impoverished Dubliners have the intellectual level akin to an oyster. I decided to write verses instead. I have often wondered why, for nobody reads them. It is a kind of disorder, an alternative and intimate form of global obscurity. Just think. What a thing it would be if all were enveloped in obscurity at this moment, the sun and the moon to go out. How terrible the idea!

CLAIRE

How unspeakably appalling! I tremble at the thought.

MARY

Stop putting silly ideas into her head. She has enough of them already.

SHELLEY

I merely conjecture cosmologically. Those little whitish specks of light that spangle the canopy of the night are, we are told, suns. Each of them is the center of a system like ours, so infinitely vast that in a future existence the soul will lose all consciousness of having formerly lived elsewhere. I do not refer to the commonly accepted delusions of Christianity, so fatal to genius and originality. I cannot accept that this great system of things, the universe, was created by a single intellectual being, remorseless, capricious and inflexible, a tyrant who made man in his own image and then damned him for being so. Never will I forgive Christianity. When I was younger I burned with impatience for its dissolution. It had injured me. I swore on the altar of perjured love to revenge myself on the hated cause.

EDWARD

And yet the vast majority of humanity, whether Christian, Muslim or Buddhist, believe devotedly in your hated cause.

SHELLEY

On what justification? Let us suppose twelve men testified before you that they had seen in Africa a vast snake three miles long. Suppose they swore that this snake ate nothing but elephants, but you knew from all the laws of nature that enough elephants could not exist to sustain the snake. Would you believe them? No, the testimony of the twelve apostles is insufficient to establish the truth of their doctrine.

MARY

Shelley is an atheist, Edward. Everyone knows that.

SHELLEY

When I was still at Oxford, I took up the word, as a knight takes up a gauntlet, in defiance of injustice.

JANE

I think I might feel too vulnerable if there were no God to believe in.

SHELLEY

On the contrary. The atheist needs no crutch to help him walk. The atheist is a monster among men. He dreads no judge but his own conscience. He fears no hell but the loss of his self-esteem. He is not to be restrained by punishments, for even death is divested of its terror.

EDWARD

So you attach no importance to how the world judges you?

SHELLEY

On the contrary, a certain degree of infamy is the best compliment which an exalted nature can receive from the filthy world of which it is its hell to be a part.

EDWARD

Most people would consider how they stand in the good opinion of society of the utmost importance.

SHELLEY

I hope you're not being serious. You remind me of what I hate and despise and shudder at – this detestable coil of primeval prejudice.

EDWARD

I was merely expressing the opinion of your own cousin.

MARY

Medwin! I can't stand him! He used to sit with us and insist on interrupting our reading or writing every moment to read all the fine things he had written. He said he intended to translate all the best passages of Dante, when he couldn't even make sense of the words. So he put in words of his own and then called them misprints. And his innumerable host of great acquaintances! He would make one believe that he attracts the great as a milk pail does flies on a summer morning.

Thomas Medwin was Shelley's second cousin. They spent their schooldays together at Syon House and later University College, Oxford. Medwin then spent some years in the Indian Army. In September 1820 he met Jane and Edward Williams in Geneva. In November he traveled to Pisa to join the Shelleys for a few weeks before going south to Naples for the winter.

SHELLEY

Mary has never been able to appreciate my poor cousin at his true value. A remarkable linguist but perhaps a little too conventional, I grant you. All those years in India hunting tigers!

MARY

A little too disposed to put into practice your own theories of free love. I can vouch for that and so can the Gisbornes.

SHELLEY

Oh, the Gisbornes! Gisborne is an excessive bore with his thin lips, receding forehead and prodigious nose, once seen never to be forgotten. It requires the utmost stretch of Christian charity to forgive. I, you know, have a little up-turned nose, my old comrade Hogg has a large hooked one. Add them both together, square them, cube them and you would have but a faint idea of the nose to which I refer.

MARY

You forget very readily what faithful friends they have been to both Claire and I on those occasions when you were not there to protect us.

SHELLEY

I am neither a watchdog nor a custodian and ceased to be a knight in shining armor a long time ago. I do little else than write poetry and not much of that.

JANE

Do you consider writing poetry a profession or a pastime?

SHELLEY

Neither one nor the other. A poet has a duty to awaken in all things that are, a community with what we experience within ourselves. Poetry is something divine, at once the center and the circumference of thought.

CLAIRE

Perhaps it is no more than destiny that creates poets.

SHELLEY

And what a destiny! Man can scarcely be so degraded that he was born only to die. If that *should* be the case, the gross and preposterous delusions of religion can hardly be supposed to exalt it. Are we no more than bubbles that rise from the filth of a stagnant pool?

EDWARD

That sounds more like hell to me.

SHELLEY

Maybe it is, and maybe we are to blame, but if God damns me even by making me my own hell, it by no means follows that I *must* desire to be so damned. I may think it extremely disagreeable, as I do to be in a bad temper, and wish to God that He would not have damned me either in this or any other way.

JANE

I hope you are not abolishing the promise of heaven altogether. That would leave us with nothing to look forward to.

SHELLEY

Those who believe that heaven is an improved version of what earth has been – a monopoly in the hands of a favored few – would do well to reconsider their opinion.

CATERINA appears on the terrace, waving her hands and pointing out to sea.

CATERINA

Il barco. L'ho appena visto.

MARY

The boat with the last of your heavy baggage is coming in. We'd better go down to the beach and supervise before they tip it all into the sea.

Without more ado she marches across the terrace and down the steps followed by everyone except Shelley, who plunges into the lecture of a book, holding it close to his eyes and slumped in his chair. After barely ten seconds he begins to slide off the chair onto the floor, where he lies curled up, the book still clasped in his hand. CLAIRE returns cautiously, kneels beside Shelley and places his head on her lap.

Scene Two: Shelley/Claire

CLAIRE

Your health seems to be very poor, my love. How is it possible to be so thin, so worn out?

SHELLEY

It is true. I am excessively weak today with much nervous irritability.

CLAIRE

You must be in love.

SHELLEY

I think one is always in love with something or other, but the love of woman is only one form of that universal love which Plato taught.

CLAIRE

Why do people love, Percy? It is sometimes such a heavy cross to bear.

SHELLEY

Of necessity love must be a desire for immortality. It is eternal.

CLAIRE

Will you love me eternally then?

SHELLEY

My dear girl, to promise to love for ever the same woman is not less absurd than to promise to believe eternally the same creed.

CLAIRE

What are you reading?

SHELLEY

Since I have read this book, I have read no other. Luxima the Indian is a perfect angel. She is perfect. It is really a divine book. It has given me strange thoughts.

CLAIRE

Will you share them?

SHELLEY

I have thought that the love, beauty and truth we seek is perhaps only in our minds.

CLAIRE

I have given you more than my mind, I think. Do you doubt that?

SHELLEY

But I cannot give in return what men call love. Mine must be the devotion of something afar, from the sphere of a shared sorrow.

CLAIRE

I can never be happy with anyone else after all that has passed between us.

SHELLEY

That time is dead for ever! Drowned, frozen, dead for ever!

CLAIRE

No! I am the same girl as ever. I have not changed, but here there is so much discontent, such violent scenes, such a turmoil of passion and hatred.

SHELLEY

It would have been better for you to have remained in Pisa.

CLAIRE

So that you can make plans with Ma behind my back as usual. I know who induced you to exile me once again. I know you, my darling. I know how you tremble whenever I come near.

SHELLEY

You know nothing, dear girl. Socrates understood that only the gods knew all things, both the things that are said and the things that are done and the things that are counseled in the silent chambers of the heart. You are not a goddess, even if I confess that your proximity troubles me excessively.

CLAIRE

We love each other. Is that forbidden?

SHELLEY

There are things we should not do or say if they were not forbidden. And yet how vain it is to think that mere words can penetrate the mystery of our being. The caverns of the mind are obscure and shadowy.

CLAIRE

Are you happy to be you?

SHELLEY

I would not be that which another is.

CLAIRE

When we three fled England together and vowed to share our love freely, I was content with our pledge.

SHELLEY

And now you are no longer content?

CLAIRE

I suppose so. I never look on you, that you do not present to my imagination the idea of an airy substance. I believe your whole life is a sigh after a more ethereal existence.

SHELLEY

I live in a world in which I move alone. I would make my bliss an infinite solitude. Where nothing is but all things seem, we are but the shadow of a dream. Had you forgotten? Last night I dreamed I was on a broad green path that wound across a plain. Wild mountains and deserts surrounded it. Yet at the same moment I was among a crowd in some imperial metropolis. Its misty shapes, pyramid, dome and tower gleamed like a pile of crags. Well, we know not where we go, nor should we seek to know. We are as clouds that veil the midnight moon.

AN INCOMPATIBLE PASSION   29

CLAIRE

The Gisbornes have been spreading rumors about us and Elena Adelaide again. Ma received a letter from Maria two days ago.

Shelley registered the birth of Elena as his daughter on December 27th, 1818 in Naples. The child was baptized on February 27th the next year and died fifteen months later.

SHELLEY

The Gisbornes are altogether the most filthy and odious animals with which I ever came in contact. In spite of ourselves, human beings like them, who surround us, infect us with their opinions. Mary is the only person to know for sure that Elena was our child. That must content the general public's thirst for scandal.

CLAIRE

You do have a great infatuation and weakness for young women, my poor Percy.

SHELLEY

The curse of life is that whatever is once known can never be unknown. You inhabit a spot for a certain time, you think you leave it, but it clings to you. I felt a deep responsibility for Elena, but she too died and left another memory to those which already tortured me. I will feel no more. It is selfish! For many months after we fled Naples, leaving Elena behind in a stranger's care, I was pursued by something. It constantly came upon me unawares. *(reciting)* "Like one, that on a lonesome road doth walk in fear and dread, and having once turned round walks on, and turns no more his head, because he knows a frightful fiend doth close behind him tread". One of the Erinyés perhaps, emerging from the castrated Uranus's drops of blood. Which one? Alecto, the unnameable. That is most befitting. Her waist entwined with serpents, her eyes dripping blood.

CLAIRE blocks her ears and tries to escape to the terrace but crumples up, moaning and sobbing hysterically. Such fits occurred frequently, induced by Shelley's visually gruesome tales. He seizes her, shakes her violently then kisses her passionately. She hangs limply in his arms.

SHELLEY

There comes a moment when we are apt to think that if this or that had not been done, such an event might have been prevented.

CLAIRE

My love was such a gentle one. He was afraid of me. I would rather have died than done him the least harm.

SHELLEY

Byron is the spirit of an angel in the mortal paradise of a decaying body. We all act a false part in the world.

CLAIRE

Where I loved the poet I should have liked to respect the man. Was that not a reasonable desire?

SHELLEY

Reason cannot know what sense can neither feel nor thought conceive. What assurances had we at the time of the tenderness of a father for his child, when he treated the feelings of the mother with so little consideration?

CLAIRE

Was it not natural that I should yearn to be constantly at my little girl's side? But he vowed that if I annoyed him again he would place Allegra in a secret convent and I would have nothing more to do with her. I tremble still to think of it and how she died there alone and abandoned. Even your intercession failed to soften him.

SHELLEY

You know how it was of vital importance both to me and yourself, to Allegra even, that I put a stop to my intimacy with L.B. I strongly suspected him of the basest insinuations. The only way I could effectively have silenced him I was reluctant to employ during my father's lifetime.

CLAIRE

You, like all the world, pay craven tribute to his rank. Surely rank and reputation are nothing in comparison to a mother's claims?

SHELLEY

What did you expect from an aristocrat? Aristocrats like Lord B are gilded flies, kept in idle comfort by the laboring poor. I could with pleasure have knocked him down after seeing his gleam of malicious satisfaction, when I told him in Venice of your declining health.

CLAIRE

While Mary I waited in Pavia to know if we had his permission to visit Allegra.

SHELLEY

We rode along the sands of the sea talking. Our conversation consisted in stories of his wounded feelings and great professions of friendship and regard for me. We talked of literary matters and his fourth canto, which he said was very good. Byron was jealous of my regard for your interests and inaccessible to all my suggestions.

CLAIRE

What wounded feelings? What regard for you? He was already dead to everything beautiful, whether of shape or essence. Already he rotted and was corrupted. The light of truth shone upon him as on a corpse putrefiying in the rays of the sun.

SHELLEY

It is not for us to judge, dear girl. We, who are so far astray. We can not even conceive whence we live, or why, or how, or what mute power may give their being to each plant and star and beast, or even these thoughts. We are chained to Time. How like death-worms the wingless moments crawl.

CLAIRE

Dearest and only love, by that love we have promised each other, although I may never be solely yours, I am exclusively yours by the kisses of love we exchange. I have pledged myself to you and that gift is sacred.

SHELLEY

Beware, Claire. All women suffer from illusions when exalting the sentiment of the passions.

CLAIRE

Am I an illusion? I think not.

SHELLEY

Everyone who knows me must know that the partner of my life should be the one who can feel poetry and understand philosophy.

CLAIRE

Philosophy! Is it philosophy that moves you when you make love to me?

SHELLEY

Carnal affection is merely making bodily the creation of fancy. Whatever strengthens the affections, enlarges the imagination and adds spirit to sense is useful.

CLAIRE

It is excessively gratifying to know that I am useful to you.

SHELLEY

You must not think I ever love you less, although that love has been and still must be a source of disquietude to me. When we are alone together, I feel that if the past and future could be obliterated, the present would content me well. I could say with Faust to the passing moment: 'Remain thou. Thou art so beautiful'

CLAIRE

How hateful it is to quarrel, to say a thousand unkind things meaning none, things produced by bitterness and disappointment. I can't think what is the matter with me lately. I weep, yet never know why. I sigh yet feel no pain. I have dreams of a child falling into a well. Another of Jane beheaded and one in which her little boy has died.

SHELLEY

When Allegra died in the convent and then William in Rome it seemed as if the destruction consuming us were as an miasma. It wrapped and infected everything connected with this dunghill of a world.

CLAIRE

It is Mary's fault. From the very beginning back in Skinner Street she was determined to seduce you. She is to blame for infecting our world. She heated your imagination by talking of her mother and going to her grave with you every day, till at last she told you she was dying of love for you. I hate her! How can you live with such a cold person?

SHELLEY

Mary's coldness is only the ash which covers an affectionate heart, but I will admit that my marital chains of lead carry greater authority than my winged words. I often feel somewhat better when away from Mary.

CLAIRE

Let us leave this prison then and join Prince Mavrocordato in Greece as you planned.

SHELLEY

You have said nothing to Mary? She is not acquainted with the project. Well, how far all this is practicable, considering the state of my finances, I do not know yet. Only be sure, dear girl, it would give me the greatest pleasure and the pleasure might be doubled or divided by your presence or absence.

MARY can be heard approaching, giving instructions to Caterina. Shelley starts up, snatches up his scattered books and papers, thrusts them into his hat and jacket pockets and makes a dash for the first floor stairs. Claire hesitates to follow him, starts too late, and is caught in the act of leaving by Mary's entry.

SCENE THREE: MARY/CLAIRE

MARY

(*entering from the terrace*)

I thought I left Percy in here.

CLAIRE

You are quite mistaken, I am sure. I have not seen the silly boy since you all went down to the beach to meet the baggage boat. I hope everything has been disembarked safely. These Italian peasants can be so remiss.

MARY

The bags are safe but already Jane pines after her own house and saucepans to which no one can have a claim except herself. It is a pity that anyone so pretty and amicable should be so selfish. We have given them a home out of charity, but gratitude seems to be a word absent from their limited vocabulary. Has Caterina found some fish for supper? With all the tumult of this morning I forgot to remind her.

CLAIRE

Percy says he cannot bear the inhumanity of Wordsworth when he talks of the beauty of the shining trout after being caught.

MARY

Indeed, he has more horror at putting a hook in a fish's mouth than giving a pang to a mother's bosom. Have you forgotten already how he obliged us to cross all Italy with Clara in that frightful state of weakness and fever, so thin you would hardly know her?

In the summer of 1818 Shelley took Claire to Padua to try and persuade Byron to return Allegra to her mother. In August he ordered Mary to cross Italy and join him, with Clara, not yet recovered from a fever a week earlier. Arriving in Florence after a hot journey on rough roads, they waited for a passport. The arduous route to Padua via Bologna took four days with Clara dangerously ill with dysentery. They all departed for Venice on September 24th. When they reached their inn, Clara was worse and died an hour later.

CLAIRE

I was dangerously ill too and so was Percy.

MARY

From taking poison in Italian cakes prescribed by that stupid fellow who called himself a medico! And you, dear sister, had a medical appointment for that unstated problem. It cannot have been another result of Byron's prolific seed this time. He had been refusing to see you for months. So my baby Clara died in that squalid inn on the lagoon, so silently and without pain, before the physician could arrive. And why? As a result of Percy's heartless efforts for you and Allegra and your unborn bastard!

CLAIRE

You have always resented that Clara died and Allegra survived. My affections for my daughter were so few and therefore so strong. The extreme solitude in which I lived away from her concentrated to one point, and that point was my lovely child. When she could hardly speak or walk, whenever she disliked anything she called out upon Papa. The violence of this disposition was discouraging and yet so mixed with affection and vivacity, I scarcely knew whether to laugh or to cry. My unhappy child was born in sorrow and after much suffering. I loved her with a passion that almost destroyed my being. Then she went from me.

MARY

William and Clara were happy children. What good did it do them?

CLAIRE

If a woman can never be happy, how can she ever bestow happiness on her children?

MARY

Oh, such an apt opinion, Miss. What happiness have you ever brought the world?

CLAIRE

You are perhaps right. I think of myself as a stranger and traveler on the earth, to whom none of the many affairs of this world belong.

MARY

How easily said! You have a tendency, partly constitutional and partly owing to the turn of your philosophy, to look with complacency on the world and its affairs.

CLAIRE

I left Venice with regret, but indeed I could not go without first having seen and embraced Allegra. I could no longer resist the feeling which haunted me that I should never see her any more. What succor did you offer to a grieving sister?

MARY

I agreed that Allegra should be separated from Byron, as remorseless as he is unprincipled. We offered to take her with us, but when Albé speaks and Shelley does not answer it is as thunder without rain, the form of the sun without heat or light, as any familiar object shorn of its dearest and best attribute. You know how my soul is entirely wrapped up in him. To see his love, his tenderness, draws tears more delicious than the smiles of love from my eyes.

CLAIRE

How true! I have only to be half an hour in his company to be convinced that there is not an atom of malevolence in his whole composition.

MARY

Last night he dreamed that he saw himself strangling me. He told me that he has had many such visions lately. He has met himself as he walked on the terrace and said to him: 'How long do you mean to be content?'

CLAIRE

Is he content?

MARY

Who knows? I would tear the veil from this perplexing world and pierce with eagle eyes beyond the sun, where every strange and unpredictable idea is another step on the ladder by which I would climb, break my chains and leave this dungeon.

CLAIRE

Has Percy spoken of a desire to leave this place? Here on this wild wind-swept coast he has reached a degree of fulfillment in his work unparalleled before, despite your constant fussing. He lets you treat him like a dog.

MARY

He knows I do not mean it.

CLAIRE

He says that a bad wife is like winter in a house.

MARY

He has no right to discuss our private life with you.

CLAIRE

It was what we agreed when I accepted to accompany you to France. You would not go without me. Have you forgotten? We agreed to share everything.

MARY

We thought we were going to die in that terrible storm then. Three nights ago, looking down the coast, I saw two great lights burning at the foce. A voice within me seemed to cry aloud that will be his grave.

She wanders out onto the terrace and gazes over the sea.

Come and look at the moon.

CLAIRE

Is there a moon already?

MARY

Yes. See it rising behind the hills.

CLAIRE

Poor fellow. *This is one of Shelley's frequent remarks and both women laugh.*

This morning I mounted the hill and sat for an hour at the foot of the ancient olive tree. Below me the groves of evergreen swayed in the high wind. The noise resembled the dashing of waves on the seashore. Being alone there with such a sound brought to my mind the many solitary hours I spent in exile in Lynmouth.

MARY

Some things are best forgotten. Be content that gentle evening has come once more. I am imagining the moon, so often friendly to me, soon at its full, rising over Venice. How many times have I looked on that scene at this hour? Sometimes I awaited S's return from the Palazzo till two or three in the morning. I watched the glancing of the oars of the gondolas. I heard their distant song and saw the palaces sleeping in the light of the moon. By its deep shadows it veiled all the grief buried in those decaying palaces. When finally I placed my head on the pillow, I did not sleep, nor could I be said to think. My imagination possessed and guided me. It gifted the successive images that arose in my mind with a vividness far beyond the usual bounds of reverie.

CLAIRE

At least you have the satisfaction of having realized some of your dreams. Edward says that all London talks of *Frankenstein*. The public packs the theaters to see it performed. The most contemptible of all lives like mine is where you live in the world and none of your passions or affections are called into action.

MARY

You always fell short of Father's expectations. Perhaps because you were only his adopted daughter.

CLAIRE

His strictness was undeviating. He was too minute in his censures, too grave and severe. He played with words without giving us the key to their interpretation. Resolve to be happy, was the essence of his advice.

MARY

You both deserve to be so! Everything that interferes with happiness is weakness and wandering.

CLAIRE

The true object of education, like that of every other moral process, is the generation of happiness.

MARY

Then Percy Bysshe Shelley, poet and philosopher, stepped over the threshold of our self-approving adolescent nest and set the cat among the pigeons.

CLAIRE

We were both only sixteen and still at school and so ready to fall in love for the first time.

MARY

But I was the one he chose to unburden his heart. Not you.

CLAIRE

He knew I would not have yielded so easily to his ardent desires. You were more compliant and gave yourself to a married man on your mother's tomb. You profaned her memory.

MARY

On the contrary, I consecrated her memory with my maidenhead. I followed her injunctions to the letter.

CLAIRE

You allowed yourself to be seduced by the first man to enter our home.

MARY

I did. Before you! In burning words Percy poured forth a tale of his wild past, how he had suffered with Harriet and her unnatural family, how he had been misled into a loveless marriage and how, if supported by my love, he hoped in future years to enroll his name with the wise and good. They had done battle for their fellow men and been true to the cause of humanity through all adverse storms. Unhesitatingly I placed my hand in his and linked my fortune with his own. Well, that was eight years ago and it is too late to debate the morality of it now.

CLAIRE

We are not responsible for the morality of a society we have relinquished. Percy says the great secret of morality is love, a going out of our own nature, an identification of ourselves with the beautiful.

MARY

Indeed, the greatest token of beauty is in our mutual love for Shelley. We who cherish him so tenderly. Whose lives hang on the beam of his eye and whose souls are entirely wrapped up in him to make him happy. *(She begins to weep)* Oh, dear! Hunt used to call me serious. What would he say to me now?

CLAIRE

What is it you want that you have not? You have the husband of your choice, to whom you are unalterably attached, a man of high intellectual endowments. You have all the goods of fortune, all the means of being useful to others. Yet all the rest of the world, all that is beautiful and all that has a claim on your kindness is nothing, just because two children are dead. *They turn back to look at the rising moon.*

MARY

Poor fellow. *This time they do not laugh.*

ACT TWO

MAY 1822

SCENE FOUR: SHELLEY/JANE

JANE is seated on the divan with a guitar on her knees. Shelley had bought her the guitar, made of pine and mahogany, encased in a box like a coffin. The guitar, he implied, contained his spirit, imprisoned like Ariel in the tree. Jane is singing a popular Sicilian love song. SHELLEY is at her knees on the floor, gazing in fixed adoration at her.

JANE

(singing)

Non dormo, né riposo a te pensando,
Passo le notti intere senza sonno,
Sempre le tue bellezze contemplanto,
Cosi passo il tempo fino a giorno,
Mi volto en mi revolto sospirando,
Mentre le mie carne non possono pui siffire.
Bella, di amare a te non provo affano,
Solo la speranza mi tiene in vita.

SHELLEY

Such tender music can produce the most overwhelming emotions. You give me excessive delight.

JANE

Flatterer. It is but a simple song, such as is sung by a multitude of star-struck Italian lovers all over the south of this country. Hardly worthy of a poet's praise.

SHELLEY

True. There is a principle within the poet's soul which acts otherwise than in a lyre. It produces not melody alone but harmony.

JANE

Your poesie, however, is not perhaps so easily accessible as my song.

SHELLEY

I can make music only for those who have the wit to understand me. A poet is a nightingale who sits in darkness and sings to cheer its own solitude. He turns all things to loveliness. He marries exultation and horror, grief and pleasure, eternity and change. He subdues to union all irreconcilable things. He transmutes all that he touches. He lays bare the naked and sleeping beauty, the very spirit of its form. A poet creates the universe anew.

He rises and walks unsteadily to a chair and sinks wearily on it.

I have been ill with an inflammatory fever and a constant pain in my side and again.

JANE

You should take more care of yourself, Mr. Poet. You hardly eat or sleep.

SHELLEY

I live like the insect that sports in a transient sunbeam, a feeble, wavering feverish being. It requires both support and consolation. I am sunk in a premature old age of exhaustion. It renders me dead to everything and gives me a terrible susceptibility to objects of disgust and hatred. But you have revived in me the expiring flame of life.

JANE

My music alone can take little credit for such a revival. You have been at work on your new poem, I think. Who gives you the inspiration you need? I hardly dare hope that it is I or my music.

SHELLEY

Poetry is the product of the poet's communion with his own mind alone. My poems are dreams of what ought to be, or may be. The mind in creation is as a fading coal. Some invisible influence, like an inconstant wind, wakens it to transitory brightness.

JANE

That does not answer my question, dissembling man. What spurs you to creation?

SHELLEY

My inspiration rises from within like the color of a flower. It fades and changes as it develops. It is a power surrounding us like the atmosphere. Some motionless lyre there is suspended and visits with its breath our silent chords.

JANE

How beautifully you express your feelings.

SHELLEY

I write all my poetry from the feelings of the moment. I shudder when I reflect how much I am in their power.

JANE

It is a dependence to be envied if it can conjure such beautiful verses.

SHELLEY

Sometimes the pressure within me throws off images and words faster than I can skim them off. My ideas come rapidly, shot through with despair and scorn of the little we can attain in our present state.

JANE

What would you attain?

SHELLEY

What I have always sought to attain. Like Saint Augustine, when I was still barely a boy, I was not yet in love with the idea of loving. I was looking for something to love, loving to love.

JANE

What do you love?

SHELLEY

I love waves and winds and storms, everything almost which is Nature's, untainted by Man's misery. I take great delight in watching the changes of atmosphere, the growth of the thunder showers which break and fade away towards evening into flocks of delicate clouds. The wind, the light, the air, the smell of a flower all affect me with violent emotions. In the motion of the meadow flowers of spring, in the blue air, I find a secret correspondence with my heart. Perhaps the flowers moralize upon their state too, have their attachments, their pursuits of virtue, adore, despond, hope, despise. Do we perish like them, or do they live like us for ever? *Quoting from his poem "Adonis".* 'The One remains, the many change and pass. Heaven's light forever shines, Earth's shadows fly. Life, like a dome of many-colored glass, stains the white radiance of Eternity'.

JANE

What a powerful image! Is it a recent work?

SHELLEY

Adonis was composed under the influence of feelings which agitated me even to tears. I think it deserves a better fate than to be linked with so stigmatized and unpopular name as mine. It is the result of a *promenade matinale* to a secluded pool, a tiny *stagno* in the pines above San Lorenzo. Like Narcissus, I lay on the mossy bank and saw my countenance reflected there. Then suddenly my youth fell from me like a wind descending on still waters. I saw my hair was prematurely gray. My face was lined with channels, such as suffering leaves behind, not age. I have had many such visions lately.

Suddenly and with great intensity Shelley draws the skin of his hands very tight and inspects them for any signs of roughness or premature aging. He leans close to Jane and places his eyes close to her neck and bosom, studying her skin minutely, as if through a magnifying glass. She gives his tousled hair an almost maternal ruffle.

JANE

I urge you, extraordinary man, to enter the slumber of the dead and the unborn. Forget all that life has imposed on you. The creators of beauty have a heavier cross to bear than common humanity.

SHELLEY

I see that in some external attributes other men resemble me. But when, misled by that appearance, I have thought to appeal to something in common and unburden my inmost soul to them, I have found my language misunderstood, like one in a distant and savage land.

JANE

Has it always been so?

SHELLEY

In my boyhood's imagination I was familiar with mountains and lakes and the sea and the solitude of forests. I was already a wanderer among distant fields. I sailed down mighty rivers. I saw the sun rise and set and the stars come forth. I saw populous cities and watched the passions which rise and spread and sink and change among the assembled multitudes of men.

JANE

With such imagination at such an early age, what place remained for the affection of loving parents?

SHELLEY

My parents have never loved me. I have always felt my mother to be mildly inadequate and narrow-minded and I have never loved my father. It is not hardness of heart, for I have loved and do love warmly, but love is the divinity that should create peace among men and my father's tyrannical rages have only reinforced my feelings about him as a rather weak and ineffectual person.

JANE

How well I understand you. I have myself had wounding and distressful experiences of tyrannical rage. Only ten days after my sixteenth birthday, I was married by arrangement to Captain Cleveland. Three days later we sailed for India. For the entire voyage he confined me to our cabin. My older brother was a general in Madras, but even he could do nothing to counter the captain's oppressive tyranny. When I met Edward at an East India Company ball, I knew immediately that I should elope with him at the first opportunity and return to England.

SHELLEY

Ah, England! Despite all its injustice and iniquity, a country dear to me forever. I felt a regret almost like remorse at leaving. The trees, the bridge at Bracknell, the minutest objects there still have a place in my affections. But I know I shall never tread its debased and degenerate soil again. The tide of destiny has washed me here and it is here I shall breathe my last.

JANE

Thoughts of death would seem premature in one so young. Even amid the tribulations of my youthful experiences, such a consideration never crossed my mind.

SHELLEY

I do not think anything of death. True horror is to be condemned to eternal earthly life, forever dragging round a worthless body, never able to rest. Not to be able to die. Not to be permitted to rest after the toils of life! Awful avenger in heaven! I do not take more than three hours of sleep and feel quite pleased at the idea that I may soon to be able to live entirely without that morbid suspension of energy.

JANE

We cannot modify the evolutionary pattern of destiny. We change as we must.

SHELLEY

I change but I cannot die.

JANE

Do you feel no fraction of the love and affection that enfolds you day after day?

SHELLEY

I only feel the want of those who can understand me. Mary does not. The necessity of concealing from her thoughts that would pain her is the curse of Tantalus. That a person possessing such excellent powers and so pure a mind should not excite the sympathy indispensable in their application to domestic life remains a mystery.

JANE

Mary strikes me in every way as being an exemplary companion. I quite envy her the chance of sharing your confidence so totally.

SHELLEY

Thank you. Mary has a greater affection for you than for anyone else. Your presence is a perpetual friendly check upon all evil.

JANE

What evil can you mean?

SHELLEY

Mary has resigned herself, especially since William's death, to a train of thoughts which, if not cut off, can only lead to some fatal end.

In May 1819 William had contracted malaria, part of the epidemic that swept Rome that year. In addition he received strong purgatives for a dangerous attack of worms. Two days later he was narrowly saved from the convulsions of death. On June 7th Shelley watched over Willliam for sixty hours without sleep until the boy died. His death devastated Mary. Only twenty-one, she had lost her third child, the son who was her most cherished offspring.

SHELLEY

Irritation at the familiar events of life are among the external marks of this inward change. Unfortunately I too am often irritable and the effect of Mary's attitude awakens in me an instinct of the power which annoys me in her. If she could be restrained from the expression of her sufferings, the sufferings themselves would subside and a new habit of sentiment take their place. But all my attempts at restraint only exasperate her more.

JANE

It seems to me, dear man, that you underestimate the affective bond between you. Both Edward and I have perceived it on many occasions.

SHELLEY

A man who lives so totally out of the ordinary world of ideas like I do needs an ever-present sympathy more than the general run of men. Mary cannot provide such sympathy in the way you do.

JANE

Now you exaggerate.

She comes and sits beside him on the divan and places her hand gently on his forehead. Softly she recites lines from a poem that Shelley had written for her when they had all lived in Pisa.

And from thy fingers flow

The powers of life, and like a sign,

Seal thee from thine hour of woe;

And brood on thee, but may not blend with thine.

Shelley trembles slightly, letting her magnetism move him, yet knowing that tranquility will never follow, for she is firmly Edward's and will never be his.

SHELLEY

Man, having enslaved the elements, remains himself a slave to his own emotions. For you alone I have reserved my highest holiest tone of love. I have plucked from the most removed and divine of strings which make music within my thoughts.

JANE

Alas! Sadly I can not, I must not, hear that particular tone.

Leaving her guitar on the divan, she hurries up the stairs to her room without a glance behind her.

SHELLEY

(to himself wistfully)

In Bracknell, while I was still hardly more than a boy, the beautiful Martha was the loveliest girl I ever saw and I loved her to distraction.

Scene Five: Shelley/Mary

MARY enters, visibly looking for something. She ferrets through the jumble of books and papers on Shelley's work desk.

MARY

It is really too vexing. I have mislaid my book, the Calderon poems I was trying to learn. I suppose you took it off in the woods somewhere and left it there as usual. *SHELLEY does not reply but it's clear from his expression that she has guessed correctly.* What a wild goose you are, Percy. Well, never mind. If my thoughts have strayed from my book, it was to the opera and my new dress from Florence, and especially the ivy wreath so much admired for my hair. And my satin slippers have not arrived. These are serious matters to gentlewomen. As to you and your ungallant companion, as it is the ridiculous custom to have men at balls and operas, I fear I must take you both with me to Pisa on Saturday. *She sees the guitar.* Jane has forgotten her instrument. I heard no music.

SHELLEY

She sang for me a while ago. The love song we heard those fishermen singing in Naples. 'Non dormo, né riposo a te pensando'.

MARY

I cannot imagine why an English lady should bother herself singing an Italian love song to another lady's husband. She will expect you to make love to her next, like all the others.

SHELLEY

Beware, Mary! Remember Marguerite of Angoulême : 'Though jealousy be produced by love, as ashes are by fire, yet jealousy extinguishes love, as ashes smother the flame.' I find Jane both amiable and beautiful, a spirit of embodied peace in our circle of tempests. She is the exact antitype of the lady in *The Sensitive Plant*, though this must be pure anticipated cognition, as the poem was written at least a year before we knew her.

MARY

I should be easier in my mind if she looked after her own husband rather than mine.

SHELLEY

Jane and Edward are not married. The gentleman whose name she bears is an obscure captain in India, a bullying brute she was lucky enough to flee.

MARY

You have the story of her life at your fingertips, I see.

SHELLEY

Jane is a delightful companion. She has a taste for music, an elegance of form and motion that compensate in some degree for a lack of literary refinement. Her singing soothes me. My nerves are generally shaken to pieces watching you others drinking until three in the morning. By dawn I am just physically well enough to crawl from the bedroom to the terrace.

MARY

Our bark is indeed tempest tossed, but love me as you ever have done.

SHELLEY

My own beloved, do I not love you? Is not your image the only consolation to my lonely and benighted condition? My mind without you is dead and cold as the dark midnight river when the moon is down.

MARY

Nevertheless, I dread Claire's being in the same house and wish the Williams were half a mile from you.

SHELLEY

The demon of distrust and pride must not be allowed to lurk between two persons in our situation. It poisons the freedom of their intercourse.

MARY

I do trust you, Percy. Most of the time. I think you are just somewhat confused.

SHELLEY

What is anyone? What is anyone not? Man is but a dream of a shadow. But when a gleam of sunshine comes as a gift from heaven, a radiant light rests on all men.

MARY

When you entered our Skinner Street home like a shooting star, I really believed you were a gift from heaven. Over the years the radiance has dimmed.

SHELLEY

Oh, there are still spirits in the air, Mary, and the genii of the evening breeze and gentle ghosts with eyes as fair as sunbeams among twilit trees. We both are in perpetual commerce with the flying clouds of stars or the deep sky and the ever-changing illumination of the air. This afternoon I lay under the wide bright blue sky. It glowed through the bare boughs of the marble-rooted fig tree. I saw, I felt its clear and piercing beams fill the universe. They impregnated the joy-inspiring wind with life and light. They cast a veil of splendor over all things, even me. There was an eloquence in the tongueless wind. It wakened my spirit to a dance of breathless rapture. It brought tears of mysterious tenderness to my eyes, like the voice of love singing to me alone.

MARY

The voice of love, my poor Percy, has lost its vibrancy. It croaks now like an old asthmatic crow. Where did you wander? I looked along the shore but saw no sign of my elusive poet.

SHELLEY

I lay in a secluded chine where the wind whispers through the winged stems of sea lavender. The waves breaking at my feet were so translucent that I could see the hollow caverns clothed with sea-moss and the leaves and branches of those delicate weeds that pave the bottom of the water. Sunbeams fell in emerald nets through the blue quivering deep like sunlight through acacia woods at dusk.

MARY

How does *The Triumph of Life* progress?

SHELLEY

Slowly. I am, I know, on the verge where words abandon us. On one day my soul is bursting. Ideas, millions of ideas, are crowding into it. Then there are days when I see nothing green any more. The grass is yellow and withered. The trees are bare. All nature seems dead in my eyes, like the hope in the bottom of my heart. What wonder if we grow dizzy to look down the dark abyss of how little we know.

MARY

From nothing, nothing can come. To nothing, nothing can return. You taught me that.

SHELLEY

What would you have me be?

MARY

What would you have yourself be?

SHELLEY

I try to be what I might have been. You know, Mary, that the poet is more delicately organized than other men. He is more sensitive to pain and suffering, both his own and that of others in a degree unknown to them.

MARY

Have we other lower beings no right to be sensitive to pain then? Since when have poets had the monopoly of pain and suffering? This obsession with poetical supremacy is becoming tiresome, Shelley. Mere intellectual condescension. You may remember that I too am an author. My awful progenitor has been admired by Byron and praised by my father.

SHELLEY

Victor Frankenstein's fantasy is but a compound of Godwin, Coleridge and Shakespeare fused in a crucible of my own invention!

As on most occasions when he begins to lose control of a situation, SHELLEY is shaken by a trembling fit and utters a piercing scream. He falls to the floor, clutching his side and drumming his heels on the carpet. MARY ignores him, picks up a book and begins reading. In a short while, SHELLEY ceases his show, pulls down a cushion from the divan and places it over his face.

SHELLEY

(Still on the floor under the cushion)

My brain has scarcely time to consult my heart or my heart to consult my brain.

MARY

Where is the love we vowed on my mother's tomb?

SHELLEY

Love withers under restraint, Mary. Its very essence is liberty. It is compatible neither with obedience, jealousy nor fear.

MARY

But those are very human attributes. How can we be otherwise?

SHELLEY

Listen to the voice of wisdom. Plato's conception of love has a universal application.

MARY

And marriage? Where does that figure in your philosophy?

SHELLEY

Marriage in its present state is a mischievous and tyrannical institution.

MARY

It is certainly a constant cause of conflict. Sometimes I think it is hateful and detestable.

SHELLEY

A kind of sickening disgust seizes my mind when I think of this most despotic fetter which prejudice has forged to confine its energies.

MARY

You consider me as a portion of yourself. You feel no more remorse in torturing me than in torturing your own mind.

SHELLEY

We torture each other. United as we are, we cannot be considered separately. Although our individual forms may move like a vain cloud through a wilderness of mountains, we are not of its shadow or its sunbeams.

MARY

Is all evolution inevitable? Can nothing divert its implacable course?

SHELLEY

All that we see or know perishes and is changed. My beloved father, unfortunately, is the living proof of the contrary.

MARY

I am sure that he has his moments of reflexion like all of us.

SHELLEY

My father has proved to my complete satisfaction that he does not think at all. He is content to follow the religion of his fathers, stupid, blind and irremediably stubborn.

MARY

Will he never make peace with us, Percy? Our union is legitimate in the eyes of his Church. Is that not enough?

SHELLEY

If he will not hear my name, I will pronounce it. He cannot think that I am an insect whom injuries destroy. Had I money enough, I would meet him in London and hollow in his ears 'Bysshe, Bysshe – aye Bysshe' until he's deaf. The real tragedy is that in many ways we are similar. Children are at best servile copies of their parents. I need not express my contempt for copies. Yet my father is so lacking in imagination that if I die tomorrow I shall have lived to be older than he. I am ninety years of age already in comparison.

MARY

I was never acquainted with your sister. Do you have no news of her?

SHELLEY

I wish you had known Elizabeth. She was a great consolation to me, but she is no longer mine. She totally rejected my love after my pamphlet on atheism. My estrangement from her together with my expulsion from Eton and my father's interdiction against returning to my family are among the great losses of my life. For more than a year I felt like a bewildered explorer of the cavern.

MARY

Is it too late to hope for a reconciliation ? I should love to know her.

SHELLEY

I fear I can never influence an amelioration now. She no longer permits an atheist to correspond with her. She talks only of duty to her father and the opinion of the world.
We were brought up to understand that unlimited passive obedience was the duty of a daughter to her parents. My mother, with some difficulty, succeeded in almost convincing me that we ought to judge for ourselves.

MARY

Perhaps no human creature ever suffered greater misery than my own mother.

SHELLEY

Now, Mary. We have been through that story a thousand times.

MARY

Tell me again, Bysshe. You know how much I need to be reminded.

She comes and sits on his lap, a little girl now, and puts her arms round his neck.

SHELLEY

No blame can be attached to you for your mother's death. You did not ask to be born. How many times have we debated this subject?

MARY

(ignoring his sighs)

Poor Fanny's father abandoned Mother for a new mistress.

SHELLEY

Oh, my goodness Mary! Must I really? Oh, very well. Your abandoned mother tried to kill herself a second time. Leaving word of where she was going, she hired a boat to row her up the river to Putney. After weighting her pockets with stones, she jumped off the wooden bridge. When Imlay's carriage arrived, her unconscious body had already been dragged from the water.

MARY

The frightened American, agreed to find a house where they could all, Mother, the baby and the mistress, live together. She agreed to this proposal.

SHELLEY

But he changed his mind and went to Paris with his mistress instead. She met your father a year later. He was a man she had already deprecated in public over his book on the rights of women. In typical fashion Godwin promised to meet this enemy as fairly as he would a friend. After an evening spent in her company, he returned home in a troubled state. It seemed painfully clear to him that the woman he had just met was in considerable anguish. He obtained her latest book and it had a profound effect on him.

MARY

He wrote to a friend that if ever there was a book calculated to make a man fall in love with its author, this appeared to him to be the book.

SHELLEY

The spell must have worked for, as a consequence, you were born. Whether from love or because of her book is a matter of conjecture.

MARY

And Mother died ten days after my birth. She seemed to believe that she would recover but Father had been informed that there was little hope.

SHELLEY

After her death Godwin set about with typical determination to find a new wife. When you were four years old he met Mrs Clairmont and her daughter, Claire. There! Are you content?

MARY

If I had not been born, Mother would still be alive today.

SHELLEY

Mary, Mary! It was the unclean hands of the doctor who delivered her that caused the infection that killed her.

MARY

Now there is a new Mrs Godwin, a woman I shudder to think of. I detest her. She plagues Father out of his life and then... well, no matter. Why won't Father follow the obvious bent of his affections and be reconciled to us? Do you not hate her, my love? What are we to do but trust to time? What else can we do? Can we not send him more money? His financial precariousness has become distressing.

SHELLEY

The considerable fortune I have already given to your father to try and save his business might as well have been thrown into the sea. I have no intention of helping him further by dipping into my patrimony. It is already too much diminished.

MARY

You agreed to go and see Mason about arranging another bill and you did not go.

SHELLEY

I dare say I am very provoking. I ought not to make appointments and not keep them. But Godwin has not once expressed any gratitude for the considerable sums I have already paid him. He has not once written to me. Even supposing I am as vile as many have supposed me, I do not see how it would injure anyone to indulge me in a little correspondence. The sun shines on many a dunghill, but its rays are so pure, so celestial, that they are never contaminated by it.

MARY

What is it that you want, my love, that you have not?

SHELLEY

Give me freedom and a place to stand on and I will move the earth! The problem is that all men, more or less, subdue themselves to the elements that surround them.

MARY

The elements that surround you here are all you have ever desired. In the olive groves and the pine woods, among the rocky pools and on the sandy shore, you are ever yourself. You can be yourself here with no one to hinder you.

SHELLEY

I am sick to death at the name of self, Mary. I am, and I desire to be, nothing.

MARY

How can you say you are nothing, silly boy! You and Lord B are the two greatest living poets. Have you no soul to be nothing?

SHELLEY

Ah, the soul! Mysterious word! Calderon saw the soul as a rock overhanging an abyss. It longs to detach itself from the dead mass of the mountain, yet dreads the fall into the unknown. I can appreciate that vision.

MARY

You once told me that the mind moves from the known to the known. It cannot reach out into the unknown. You cannot think of something you do not know.

SHELLEY

Well done! You are becoming quite a metaphysician, my love. Let us leave the unknown to its own business for the moment and think of something we know. My thoughts still cling to Windsor Forest and the copses of Marlow, and the clouds which hang upon the hills, low and trailing. Though they pass away, they leave their dew, when they themselves have eternally faded.

MARY

You cannot catch the eternal in the net of time through memory, can you? Eternity, the timeless, can surely only be when memory has ceased totally? In any case our happiness is not the product of time. Happiness is always in the present. Let us be always happy, my love.

SHELLEY

Do you know what my greatest content would be? To desert all human society. I would retire with you and our surviving child to a solitary island in the sea, build a boat and shut the floodgates of the world upon our retreat. To the alone life is eternal.

MARY

But you are not alone, Percy! You have a wife who loves society and a child who needs contact with other children. What will we do on your solitary island?

SHELLEY

You may do what you choose to do.

MARY

Dear God! All your life you have remained unaware of your ability to hurt and damage the countless women with whom you come in contact and profess to love.

SHELLEY

What women have I hurt and damaged?

MARY

The list is long. Do you need it? Emilia was the last, it seems to me. Or has there been someone since who has escaped my vigilance? Oh, Jane, of course. Let us not forget Jane and her angelic singing!

SHELLEY

My kind of love for Jane and Emilia is not the same as what you and Claire call love. Visiting Emilia in her convent prison enchanted me infinitely. I soothed myself with the idea that I made the discomfort of her captivity lighter by the demonstration of the interest she awoke in me.

MARY

Interest indeed! My friendship ended with her request for money. It put me in mind of the nursery rhyme about the pretty maid on Cranbourne Lane. After being given cakes and wine she asked for brandy.

SHELLEY

How in your opinion she must be fallen from the boasted purity in which you knew her once exulting when you first met.

MARY

Purity indeed! The virtuous virgin incarcerated between those high convent walls, waiting to be saved. My poor Shelley! Did you never for a moment see that Emilia's virtue was but a cunning calculation, a clever adjustment to her hostile environment? That virtue was only an escape from her own pettiness. And you believed her! Just as you believe Claire whenever she proclaims her everlasting love and then trips blissfully into Byron's bed.

SHELLEY

Have you been rebuking the poor girl again? She is very sullen today.

MARY

That is because she must return soon to Florence. The Masons have been calling for her services again and we can hardly afford to pension her eternally. Well, never mind Claire, my love. We are happy.

SHELLEY

How I would like you and your sister to live together on better terms.

MARY

She is not my sister. We have neither the same mother or father. She arrived in Skinner Street attached to Mrs Clairmont's apron strings.

SHELLEY

I think she has a sincere affection for you.

MARY

I have a very sincere affection for my own Shelley.

SHELLEY

Well, we all have power over ourselves to do and to suffer. What, we do not know until we try.

MARY

If we ever quarrel, which is seldom, it is I not Claire who is harsh and our instantaneous reconciliations are sincere and affectionate.

SHELLEY

Let us make the best of it, then. Living in the same home can be a wearisome lot. When love fails all is lost.

MARY

Unless it can be revived. Indeed, I will be a good girl and never vex you more.

She trips coquettishly over the terrace and down the steps. SHELLEY returns to his book, holding it close to his eyes as usual. He hears MARY'S voice off-stage talking to a man and dives under the table without ceasing to read.

EDWARD TRELAWNY enters from the terrace. He is a handsome, dashing, quixotic man of thirty with an unruly mop of black hair, a drooping mustache and a wisp of black hair under his lower lip. He had served with the Royal Navy in India and met the Shelley's in Pisa. Later he was to accompany Byron to the Greek War of Independence. He had considerable personal magnetism but, as Mary later said was "a strange, wonderful being destroyed by being nothing."

SCENE SIX: SHELLEY/TRELAWNY

TRELAWNY

(peering under the table)

Is this your study?

SHELLEY

Yes, and these are my books. They tell no lies.

TRELAWNY

Do some people tell you lies?

SHELLEY

Oh, yes. "Their delight is in lies. They give good words with their mouth, but curse with their heart." Psalm 62.

He emerges from under the table, goes onto the terrace, spreads his arms, and gazes out over the bay.

What a glorious world! There is, after all, something worth living for, which makes me retract the wish that I had never been born.

TRELAWNY

It is a delightful spot you have found, I must admit. What do you do to pass the time, when you are not gazing at this divine bay?

SHELLEY

We read Spanish dramas and listen to the most enchanting music. My only regret is that the summer must ever pass and that Mary has not the same predilection for the place as I have.

TRELAWNY

Few women can find fulfillment far from the city and the thrills of society. We are, after all, social entities as well as individuals.

SHELLEY

But society does not offer freedom of inspiration to the individual. There. You are now sitting on the stool of inspiration. In those three olive trees the weird sisters are imprisoned and this sea at our feet is their cauldron of black broth. The Pythian priestesses uttered their oracles from below. Now they are muttered from above. Listen to the solemn music in the pine tops. Don't you hear the mournful murmurings of the sea? Sometimes they rave and roar, shriek and howl like a rabble of priests. In a storm, when a ship sinks out there in the bay, we catch the despairing groans of the drowning mariners. Their chorus is the eternal wailing of wretched men. Isn't life and the world is an astonishing thing? The great miracle. What are changes of empires, the wreck of dynasties, the birth and extinction of religions and political systems compared to life? What is the universe of stars and suns, their motions, their destiny compared with life?

TRELAWNY

And the soul? What role does it play in your scheme of things?

SHELLEY

Ah, the soul! Another mystery. We want to know our soul because we have lost the song in our heart and so we pursue the singer and ask him whether he can teach us how to sing.

TRELAWNY

Do you believe in the immortality of the soul?

SHELLEY

Certainly not! How can I? We know nothing about it. We have no evidence. We cannot even express coherently our inward thoughts. If you know any gentleman personally acquainted with his soul, pray ask him from me how one is to get at it.

TRELAWNY

Why do you call yourself an atheist?

SHELLEY

It is just a word of abuse to stop discussion, a painted devil to frighten the foolish, a threat to intimidate the wise and good. I use it to express my abhorrence of superstition. I took up the word as a knight takes up the gauntlet in defiance of injustice and the delusions of Christianity.

TRELAWNY

How so? I would have said that Christ had precious few delusions.. Which is, no doubt, why they crucified him.

SHELLEY

Christ was a nonconformist and a rebel. As a person he has always attracted me, but I loathe the system the Church has established of inculcating the truth of Christianity and the excellence of the monarchy by such equivocal arguments as confiscation and imprisonment, invective and slander. With insolence it violates the most sacred ties of nature and society.

TRELAWNY

Nothing is ideal. We have little choice but to live with what religion and politics serve us. Neither ever hindered me from living life to the full.

SHELLEY

I once thought to study politics but was glad when my good genius said refrain. I see little virtue in public life. The contest is one of blood and gold. Over two thousand years ago Plato understood that there could be no place in the world of politics for an honest man.

TRELAWNY

Do you consider yourself honest?

SHELLEY

Most certainly! But my honesty has seldom brought me anything but reproach and condemnation. Perhaps I should have shrunk from persisting in the task I undertook in early life. I opposed myself in those evil times and among evil tongues to what I esteemed misery and vice. At the time I leaped headlong into the sea of society. I became better acquainted with the depths, the quicksands and the rocks than if I had stayed upon the green shore, piped a silly tune and taken tea and comfortable advice. As a result I have been dragged before the tribunals of tyranny and superstition to answer with my children, my property, my liberty and my fame for having exposed their frauds.

TRELAWNY

You exaggerate, surely. Your fame is assured and your liberty undisputed.

SHELLEY

But not my children! Sequestered by the loathed Westbrooks, damn them! Cast into the arms of Harriet's unmentionable sister.

TRELAWNY

Did no one propose placing them in the custody of their grandfather?

SHELLEY

It was too late to appeal to my father's love for me, so I appealed to his duty to the God whose worship he professed. He refused. I appealed to the terrors of that day which he believed to seal the doom of mortals. He quavered but stood firm. My father has always regarded me as a blot, a defilement of his honor. Before we left England he diminished my allowance to a mere pittance. He wished to reduce me to poverty and accept some commission in a distant regiment. He hoped I would die for king and country in the Peninsular Wars. My mother valued the happiness of my father more than the opinion of mankind or the safety of her only son. I need hardly say how frivolous that is.

TRELAWNY

I served my king and country for five years. My one regret is that I just missed being at Trafalgar. My last ship, the frigate *Cornelia* returned from Java two weeks after the battle.

SHELLEY

A half-witted Hanoverian! God Lord, Tré. How can you call that a king? You know my passion for a republic or anything which approaches it. The system of society as it exists in England is an engine, perpetually wearing away and breaking into pieces the wheels of which it is composed. It must be overthrown from the foundations and modern European society with it!

TRELAWNY

You are, no doubt, what people are beginning to call a democrat, whatever that means. The right for freedom and a vote for all.

SHELLEY

Heavens, no! To extend the vote to all would be to place the power in the hands of men who have been rendered brutal, stupid, torpid and ferocious by ages of slavery. Their savage brutality is proportional to the arbitrary character of their government.

TRELAWNY

You are very harsh on poor old England. Have you forgotten Waterloo?

SHELLEY

You are a military man, Tré. I have neither interest no respect for such activities. I can only perceive, to my great shame, that the majority of people in England are destitute and miserable, ill-clothed, ill-fed and ill-educated. As for the government, the House of Commons is a hospital for lunatics and the monarchy only a string which ties the robber's bundle.

TRELAWNY

Surely not all the ruling class are robbers. Our government cannot be entirely rotten.

SHELLEY

Conscience is the only government before which all others sink into nothingness. But in any case, as you well know, I am one of those whom nothing will satisfy. I fear that I am hardly human any more. I used to be. As a boy I rode on horseback accompanied by Lucas, my father's steward, giving money to the poor and asking Lucas for more when I ran out. Now you might as well go to a gin shop for a leg of mutton than expect anything earthly from me. I had all that drained out of me at school. Sion House Academy can boast of having transformed me from an emotionally sensitive small boy into a flailing whirlwind of violent and extremely excitable temper. The least circumstance that thwarted me produced the most violent paroxysms of rage. I would pick up anything, even any little boy who chanced to be near me, to throw at my tormenters. I was once driven to pinning a boy's hand to the desk with my knife. Many considered me on the borders of insanity. Sion House was a perfect hell to me.

TRELAWNY

We have much in common then. My unhappy school days in Bristol ended in my being expelled for violent behavior towards my teachers. I also expressed my indignation at the daily floggings inflicted on all of us by starting fires in the most unexpected places.

SHELLEY

And I blew up my desk with home-made gunpowder in the middle of a most bothersome history lesson about Malthus. The wretched teacher was defending a heinous philosophy that advocated taking from the poor the one thing which made it impossible to degrade them below beasts, the soothing, elevating and harmonious gentleness of sexual intercourse. Malthus had the insolence to propose that they abstain, while the rich are permitted to add as many mouths to consume the products of the labor of the poor as they please.

TRELAWNY

The explosion must have won you considerable prestige among your fellow pupils.

SHELLEY

I was adored by my age-mates, but the older boys and masters disliked me. They deemed me as ranging between madness and folly. It suited me well enough. It allowed me to keep at a safe distance from the prevailing propensity for perverse practices that dominate our public school system. It only prevents men from being corrupted by the world by corrupting them before their entry into the world. A public schoolboy is allowed to indulge with impunity in practices which, when he leaves school, would consign him to hard labor.

TRELAWNY

I fear that Lord B took greater advantage of the opportunity than you did. I consider myself a hardened mariner not easily shocked, but Byron's licentious lifestyle would make the most profligate of libertines blush.

SHELLEY

Byron has many generous and exalted qualities but the canker of aristocracy wants to be cut out. He is familiar with the lowest sort of women. He allows fathers and mothers to bargain with him for their daughters. He associates with wretches who seem almost to have lost the gait and physiognomy of humans. They avow to practices which are not only named but I believe seldom ever conceived in England. And none of these unmentionable practices seem to trouble his conscience.

TRELAWNY

His lameness certainly helps to make him skeptical, cynical and savage. The Italian women he musters seem oblivious to his defects.

SHELLEY

Italian women are contemptible, ignorant, disgusting, bigoted and filthy, far removed from beauty or grace. Except in the dark, there can be no peril. Countesses smell so much of garlic that an ordinary Englishman cannot approach them.

They are a mixture of the coquette and prude, the worst characteristics of English women. They are, however, better than the men, a tribe of stupid and shriveled slaves without a gleam of intelligence. I detest all society, almost all at least, and Lord Byron is the nucleus of all that is hateful and tiresome in it. His conduct with Claire wore an aspect of great cruelty, yet he persists in justifying it to himself.

TRELAWNY

Come now, Shelley! You of all people know very well that if an attractive girl of eighteen comes prancing to you at all hours, there is but one way out.

SHELLEY

He wounded us both deeply. How deep his wounds cut me you can hardly conjecture. Certain it is that Lord Byron has made me feel bitterly the inferiority which the world has presumed to place between us. It subsists nowhere in reality but in our own talents. These are not our own but Nature's. Our rank is not our own but fortune's. How long the alliance between the snake and the eagle may continue I will not prophesy. Incidentally, I am told that the magazines in England blaspheme me at a great rate. But for my detractors I should be utterly unknown.

TRELAWNY

But for them Williams and I should never have crossed the Alps in chase of you. Our curiosity as sportsmen was excited to see and have a shot at so strange a monster as they represented you to be.

SHELLEY

And what is your verdict?

TRELAWNY

As a curiosity or as a poet?

SHELLEY

Whichever you consider the most consequential.

TRELAWNY

As a poet then. *The Triumph of Life* is superior to anything Byron has produced.

SHELLEY

If that be true, it is only because Byron makes no effort. Should he do so, his poetry would be of a level unparalleled since Shakespeare. I shall lose no sleep over Lord B's future successes. I have the vanity to write only for poetical minds and must be satisfied with few readers. Byron is ambitious. He writes for all and all read his works.

TRELAWNY

He is turning his hand to drama now. John Murray, his patron and paymaster, says Byron's plays won't act. Byron doesn't mind that. He told Murray his plays were not written for the stage. But he added his poesie wouldn't sell either. That he does mind, for he has an itching palm. Murray is urging him to resume his old Corsair style to please the ladies.

SHELLEY

Very good logic for a book seller but not for an author. The shop's interest is to supply the ephemeral demand of the day. It is not for Murray but Byron to put a ring in the monster's nose to keep him from mischief.

TRELAWNY

I suspect that Murray is right, if not righteous. All Byron has yet written has been for women. Let us wait until he is forty. Their influence will then die a natural death and he will show the men what he can do.

SHELLEY

He should do it now and write nothing but what his conviction of its truth inspires him to write. He should give counsel to the wise, not take it from the foolish. Time will reverse the judgment of the vulgar. Contemporary criticism only represents the amount of ignorance genius has to contend with.

TRELAWNY

His *Don Juan* was cast aside and almost forgotten until the pharisaic synod in John Murray's back parlor pronounced it as highly immoral and unfit for publication.

SHELLEY

In Murray's back parlor they discourse on the morals of a whore with the manners of a dancing master.

TRELAWNY

Maybe few people read your verses but I'm glad to see that the Snake can still bite. The day before I left Byron, he received another anonymous letter warning him against you. Many people, it would seem, consider you a public danger.

SHELLEY

That is because I alone in this age of humbug dare stem the current, as I did on the flooded Arno.

TRELAWNY

Although we could not observe you made any phenomenal progress.

SHELLEY

The attempt, at least, was better than being swept along as all the rest with the filthy garbage scoured from its banks.

TRELAWNY

'If we puffed out the Snake', Byron once told me, 'it might not turn out a profitable investment. If Shelley cast off the slough of his mystifying metaphysics, he would want no puffing.' Why not get Byron to join you here? With your family and the Williams and books and horses and the boat, undisturbed by the botheration of the world, you shall have all that reasonable people require. Propose it to him.

SHELLEY

No, you must do that. Byron is always influenced by his last acquaintance. You are the last man, so you pop the question. In any case, as long as Claire chooses to remain here, there can be no question. Her temper, like Mary's, is easily crossed.

TRELAWNY

Is Miss Clairmont thinking of leaving?

SHELLEY

Not if I were asked to offer an opinion. Mary, however, has other priorities. Ah, before I forget and we are disturbed, I would consider it a great kindness if you could procure me a small quantity of prussic acid or essential oil of bitter almonds. It requires the greatest caution in preparation and ought to be highly concentrated. Not a word to the girls. It would only cause a monumental fuss. I will give any price for this medicine. Rest assured, I have no intention of suicide at present, but it will comfort me to own this golden key to the chamber of perpetual rest.

TRELAWNY

You would be sadly missed.

SHELLEY

You are too romantic, Tré. When a man marries, dies or turns Hindu, his best friends hear no more of him. My mind is tranquil. I have no fears and some hopes. When death removes our clay coverings, the mystery will be solved. Have you any news from Roberts?

TRELAWNY

The mast has arrived. If you wish him to fit it, the *Don Juan* must be sailed back to the yard.

SHELLEY

In a week or two. As soon as the wind veers north again and stays there for a few days, we shall make the trip. Will you send him a message to that effect?

TRELAWNY

Willingly. The young Vivian lad can ride over this afternoon. Let me arrange it. *He exits to undertake his mission.*

Scene Seven: Shelley/Mary/Jane/Edward/Claire

EDWARD *enters holding a paper, a poem that Shelley has recently addressed to Jane.*

EDWARD

Jane begs me to say that she can not answer your kindness in person. As for my movements, I am going to shoot this evening. That is, I feel I must parade you at ten paces, if you go on sending my wife poems in this way. If you will call yourself, or send your second, we will point out the ground.

SHELLEY

A man has a right to think, to feel and to speak. He will feel. He must speak and he ought to express those thoughts and feelings with the readiest sincerity and the strictest candor.

EDWARD

Even if it entails a loss of respect in the eyes of his friends?

SHELLEY

No man has the right to be respected for any other possession but those of virtue and talent, and no law has the right to discourage the practice of truth. A man ought to speak the truth on every occasion. At any rate you should not seek for such a model among men of the pen. We are too thick-skinned and egotistical.

CLAIRE and JANE enter with flowers they have picked. They arrange them in vases.

CLAIRE

Truth lies at the bottom of a well. Had you forgotten, Percy?

SHELLEY

Not I, dear girl!

CLAIRE

One day in Naples, the silly boy jumped down the well in the courtyard outside our villa. He wanted to ascertain if the proverb were correct. Alas, the well shaft narrowed three feet down and he got stuck.

JANE

Were you very disappointed that the well kept its secret?

SHELLEY

Not in the least. The world needs its secrets. How came the universe at first, for example? A materialist will answer 'by chance' In the words of Spinoza 'an infinite number of atoms had been floating for all eternity in space. At last one of the diverged from its track. Dragging with it another atom, it formed the principle of gravitation and in consequence the universe'. And the secret? What cause produced this change? Surely some?

JANE

I am certain that you have the key to the mystery.

SHELLEY

Was not this then the soul of the universe, the spirit of universal love? Indeed I believe it.

MARY

(entering)

Universal love! When you say you love someone, Percy, do tell us what exactly you mean?

EDWARD

He means that love is possession.

SHELLEY

Certainly not! When you know how to love one, you know how to love the whole not an individual. When you love, there is neither one nor many. There is only love.

CLAIRE

(almost in a trance)

How true! I feel love like a remembered dream. I am a part and yet everything at the same time. I turn the corner of a lane and the view, which its high banks and hedges has concealed, presents itself. It consists of a windmill standing among plashy meadows enclosed with stone walls. A long low hill rises behind the windmill and a gray covering of uniform cloud spreads over the evening sky. It is the season when the last leaf has just fallen from the scant and stunted ash trees. The scene surely is a common scene, but I suddenly remember to have seen that exact scene in some dream of long ago. I stand in a trance, which is not slumber. The shade it spreads is so transparent that the scene comes through as clear as when a veil of light is drawn over evening hills. They glimmer and I know I have already felt the freshness of that dawn. I have bathed in the same cold dew as clings to my brow and hair. I have once before sat upon that slope under the self same bough.

SHELLEY

Wake the serpent not, Claire, lest he should not know the way to go. Let him crawl creeping through the deep grass.

MARY

Stop it, Shelley!

SHELLEY

(ignoring her)

A great old snake, perhaps my ancestor, lived in our garden in the reign of James 1, nine feet long, equipped with squat legs and primitive wings. Sometimes it slithered to the very edge of the lake and lawns. Seemingly endless and viscous, it slid silently from the rampant vegetation in search of an unsuspecting prey.

CLAIRE begins to show the usual signs of fearful agitation, moaning and writhing on her chair.

MARY

Leave the silly girl alone, Shelley!

SHELLEY

Mary, you can hardly expect me to behave with the courtliness of my esteemed family. I am an ardent disciple of Plato, who considered good birth and fame and all such distinctions as showy ornaments of vice. Lord B is a matchless example. I merely tread in the steps of the master.

EDWARD

Surely you do not denigrate your ancestors? The aristocracy is the backbone of English supremacy.

SHELLEY

A pitiful supremacy! The aristocracy condemn all but their first-born to starvation and place in his hands the rod of despotism. I am one of these aristocrats. In me the same machinery of oppression is preparing in order that I in my turn may become an oppressor.

MARY

We had great hope that a longer intercourse with Shelley would operate to weaken those superstitions of rank and wealth which Lord Byron, in common with other aristocrats, is so poisonously imbued.

SHELLEY

But my father deceives himself. My first act, when in possession of my estate, shall be to divide it equally with my family, unnatural as it may be.

JANE

Just to spite your father?

SHELLEY

Certainly! Once when I was very ill during the holidays, recovering from a fever which had attacked my brain, a servant overheard my father consult about sending me to a private madhouse. I was a favorite among all our servants, so this fellow came and told me, as I lay sick in bed. My horror was beyond words. I might soon have gone mad indeed if my father had proceeded in his iniquitous plan. Later, when the Courts took my two children away from me, hate grew within me of the many crimes, the harsh and grating strife of tyrants. I longed to see my sister, Elizabeth, and wished that vile family despotism and the viler despotism of religion did not stand between the happiness of two beings. She will now, I fear, never more return the affection which would once again bid me be happy. Such are the deleterious effects of religious education.

EDWARD

Not all poets are atheists. The week we left London, Blake's *Everlasting Gospel* appeared in the bookshops.

JANE

He is so eccentric but quite brilliant and as mad as his paintings.

SHELLEY

On the contrary, the sanest of men. A man without a mask, his aim single, his path straightforwards and his wants few. In short, free, noble and happy, unlike the rest of us. Blake belongs to a era when men saw beauty shining in pure light, not bearing the marks of that thing we carry around and call the body, imprisoned in it like an oyster in its shell.

CLAIRE

Surely we are not all imprisoned in a shell, Percy?

MARY

You are not a poet, silly girl. How can you understand?

SHELLEY

A poet in our times is a semi-barbarian in a civilized community. He lives in the days that are past. His ideas, thoughts, feelings, associations are all with barbarous manners, obsolete customs and exploded superstitions. The march of his intellect is like that of a crab, backwards. The brighter the light diffused around him by the progress of reason, the thicker is the darkness of antiquated barbarism, in which he buries himself like a mole.

JANE

Dear me, all this talk of oysters, crabs and moles! We have lost sight of the poet.

EDWARD

What is a poet, Shelley?

SHELLEY

A poet is the unacknowledged legislator of the world, a hierophant, an expounder of the sacred mysteries. He is the mirror of gigantic shadows, cast by the future upon the present with words which express what they do not understand. The trumpets which sing to battle fail to feel what they inspire. The poet beholds intensely the present as it is. His thoughts are the germs of the flower and fruit of latest time.

EDWARD

I fear we simple mortals may have some difficulty following such abstruse arguments. Can you not be more practical?

SHELLEY

The ancient Greek legislators used poetry to subdue the savage nature of the people. As Plato says of music, poetry penetrates the recesses of the soul. It seemed to him to be the most powerful means of instructing youth. I would often read my verses to William. Although he would understand very little, the musical intonations soothed him.

MARY

He was so very delicate. We had to take the greatest possible care of him in summer.

SHELLEY

The torrid Italian weather indisposed him extremely.

MARY

We were fools to remain in Rome all that time, Rome noted for malaria, the famous caterer of death.

SHELLEY

Despite the oppressive heat, he had lost all shade of ill temper and become affectionate and sensible to an extraordinary degree.

MARY

It was impossible to find a creature more gentle and intelligent. His health and strength appeared to be perfect. His beauty, the silken fineness of his hair, the transparency of his complexion, the animation and deep blue of his eyes were the astonishment of everybody. The Italian women used to bring each other to look at him when he was asleep. Oh, dear, I shall begin weeping again.

EDWARD

(*anxious to change the subject*)

Where has our Cornish buccaneer gone?

SHELLEY

Roberts has sent word that he is ready to proceed with work on the *Don Juan*. Tré is gone to organize the affair. Last night I dreamed of nothing but sailing and fishing up coral.

MARY

Trelawney's company is delightful. He excites one to think.

CLAIRE

But he is so excessively extravagant. And then there is his air of extreme good nature. It pervades his whole countenance, especially when he smiles. It assures me that his heart is good.

MARY

He tells such strange stories of himself, horrific ones that harrow one up.

JANE

With his simple yet strong language he portrays the most frightful situations.

EDWARD

And apparently all these adventures in the East took place between the ages of thirteen and nineteen, when he left the Navy.

CLAIRE

I believe them now I have seen the man.

EDWARD

Had you not known him in Pisa, Miss Clairmont?

MARY

I loathe Pisa A most ugly town. The ladies there dress in dirty cotton gowns. They wear soiled white satin shoes. They hide their faces under huge bonnets of pink silk with bows perched on the points of their chins. The men are surly fellows with bushy hair, large whiskers, canes in their hands and a bit of dirty colored ribbon sticking in their buttonholes.

CLAIRE

They mean to look like the lords of the rabble but only look like their drivers.

MARY

We all lost our hearts to Naples, despite the heat and the dirt.

SHELLEY

(reciting from his Ode to Naples)

"I stood within the city disinterred and heard the autumnal leaves like light footfalls of spirits passing though the streets, and heard the Mountain's slumberous voice at intervals thrill through those roofless halls."

CLAIRE

How perfectly true! In the wild woods surrounding Pompeii you hear the late leaves of autumn shiver and rustle in the stream of inconstant wind, as it were like the step of ghosts.

EDWARD

Did you hear the Mountain's slumberous voice at first hand?

CLAIRE

Only Percy reached the crater rim. The climb is too strenuous for ladies.

SHELLEY

Standing in a black shower of ashes on the volcano's summit, I observed the lava creep on perpetually with the crackling sound of suppressed fire.

JANE

Well, I personally consider Florence the most beautiful city, when the sea winds sweep through the streets and past the sleeping palaces.

CLAIRE AND SHELLEY

(reciting together)

"Oh, wild west wind, thou breath of autumn's being, from whose unseen presence the dead leaves are driven like ghosts from an enchanter fleeing."

SHELLEY

The poem was conceived in a wood that skirts the Arno near Florence on a day of tempestuous wind. It was collecting the vapors which pour down with the autumnal rains at sunset. Later there was a violent tempest of hail, attended by that magnificent thunder and lightning so peculiar to the Cisalpine regions.

JANE

Have you progressed with the drama you promised us? What was the story? I seem to have forgotten.

MARY

An Enchantress, that is my role, living in one of the islands of the Indian Archipelago saves the life of a Pirate, and that is your role Edward, a man of savage but noble nature.

JANE

Most suitable, my dear.

MARY

She becomes enamoured of him. He, inconstant to his mortal love, for a while returns her passion. At length, recalling the memory of her whom he left, and who laments his loss, he escapes from the enchanted island and returns to his lady.

JANE

Suppose I choose not to have him back?

SHELLEY

Of little consequence. His mode of life makes him go again to sea and the Enchantress seizes the opportunity to bring him back to her island in a spirit-brewed tempest. That little piece, however will have to wait. I am being hard pressed to finish the Greek drama. My investigations have led me to the conclusion that the Grecian gods seem indeed to have been more innocent than we assume. It cannot be said, however, that as far as temperance and chastity are concerned, they gave so edifying an example as their successors. There is no book which shows the Greeks precisely as they were. They seem all written for children with the caution that no practice or sentiment inconsistent with our present manners should be mentioned.

EDWARD

Surely Plato provides us with ample evidence as to the Greek way of life?

SHELLEY

In many particulars the *Symposium* shocks our present manners. No one can be a reader of the works of antiquity unless they can transport themselves to those earlier times and not judge by our but their morality. The very notion of morality has changed since the Athens of Plato and Socrates. Greek male lovers, for example, achieved sexual gratification by using fantasies. For the Greeks, pederasty was more than a sexual pastime or preference. It was a sacred institution. A relationship between an older man and a beardless boy was a cultural ideal. The relationship was regarded as mutually beneficial. The older man educated, protected, loved and provided a model for his boy lover, who in turn offered his partner beauty, youth, admiration and love.

JANE

It is hardly a suitable subject for the average English reader.

SHELLEY

Unfortunately, the laws of modern composition do not permit a modest writer to investigate such a sensitive subject with any philosophical accuracy. The Greeks were a divine people. In their very errors they are the mirrors, as it were, in which all that is delicate and graceful contemplates itself. They believed that those who do not love their fellow beings, be they male or female, live unfruitful lives and prepare a miserable grave for their old age.

Suddenly he shrieks, puts his hands to his head as if suffering from a terrible headache and makes a dash for the terrace. Edward, sitting nearest the windows, blocks his path and retains him. Mary and Claire, accustomed to these fits, each slap his cheek violently twice.

CLAIRE

Have you had visions again, dear? Never mind. They will pass.

MARY

The silly man imagines that he sees a naked woman who has eyes instead of nipples. Whoever heard of such nonsense?

EDWARD

Indeed? Eyes in the place of nipples? Most unorthodox!

MARY

Well, Jane and I are off to the village together. We shall talk morality and pluck violets by the way.

They pick up their bonnets and parasols and exit across the terrace.

CLAIRE

(still holding him)

Mary is adamant that I return to Florence tomorrow. When shall we see each other again?

SHELLEY

Forget me, dear girl, and do not revive past things. Above all take care of yourself.

They kiss passionately, as if knowing it is for the last time, that they will never meet again.

ACT THREE

JULY 1822

SCENE EIGHT: SHELLEY/TRELAWNY

SHELLEY is alone at his desk, searching for something among the pile of papers. Visibly harassed, he scratches his head, kneels by the table fumbling through more papers on the floor. TRELAWNY appears on the terrace.

TRELAWNY

Have you found it?

SHELLEY

I have lost it. I have lost a whole day.

TRELAWNY

Cheer up, my lad and come down to dinner.

SHELLEY

You go. I have dined. Late eating don't do for me.

TRELAWNY

What's this? *(He uncovers a plate from beneath the papers)*

SHELLEY

That? Why, that must be my dinner. It is very foolish. I thought I had eaten it.

TRELAWNY

It is small wonder you lost sight of it, buried under reams of writing.

SHELLEY

You must know that I either am or fancy myself something of a poet.

TRELAWNY

What have you turned your hand to now that the Greek play is finished?

SHELLEY

I feel too little certainty of the future and too little satisfaction with regard to the past to undertake any new subject seriously and deeply. I stand, as it were, upon a precipice. I have ascended with great peril and cannot descend without greater. I am content if the heaven above me is calm for the passing moment.

TRELAWNY

Surely you will not disappoint your disciples by snuffing out the candle of your genius?

SHELLEY

Certainly not! I always go on until I am stopped. And I am never stopped. I am as a spirit who has dwelt within a poet's heart. I have felt his feelings and have thought his thoughts and known the inmost converse of his soul. With my verses I try to convince that pig, the public, to desert its cherished mud. I offer a drop of dew, a tiny libation of light and nobody reads me. It is a sort of disorder.

TRELAWNY

Yet a multitude of voices, albeit discreet, rise daily in praise of your sublime songs.

SHELLEY

What I can neither see nor feel, I can not trust. I seek the truth, like the pebble in the lake. It sends ripples right to the rim, from the still pure center to the circumference, like the steady turning outwards of the self to the other.

TRELAWNY

Which other?

SHELLEY

There lies the contradiction. In his search for the truth, the self is attempting to BE something – to be noble, to be good, to be virtuous, to be happy -but in this desire to BE something, there is a contradiction – not to be something else.

TRELAWNY

The grass is always greener on the other side of the hill.

SHELLEY

And the reflection in the canal more beautiful than the objects it reflects. Why?

TRELAWNY

We live in the hope of an eventual transmutation.

SHELLEY

What is hope? Nothing but the paint on the face of existence! The universe has probably always existed and will go on operating immutably, according to the laws of its own nature. There's your transmutation!

TRELAWNY

Hope is a matter of principle. The desire for improvement is what we all aspire to. Surely, there is no great extravagance in presuming that there should be a perfect identity between the moral and physical improvement of the human species?

SHELLEY

Until the mind can love and admire and trust and hope and endure, reasonable principles of moral conduct are but seeds cast upon the highway of life. The unconscious passenger tramples them into dust. A friend of mine once told me that his father had invited some corporation to dine at his house and that he was present. When the dinner was over and the gentlemen nearly drunk, they swore they would all kiss his sisters. His father laughed and did not forbid them. The wretches would have done it, but his sisters overheard the infamous proposal and locked themselves in their bedrooms. It seems to me that a man of spirit ought to have killed them, if they had accomplished their purpose.

TRELAWNY

Your censorious attitude bewilders me. I had been led to believe that you were an ardent admirer of the fair sex. In my case, I can hardly castigate such manners after years in the Orient. The brothels of Java and Bombay hold no mysteries for me. Unlike you, I never acquired the refinements of an Oxford quad.

SHELLEY

Wrong again, Tré! Oxonian society was insipid to me, uncongenial with my habits of thinking. I could not descend to such common life. Fortunately, Mary shares my views on social proprieties, but hers is a sad fate. She can't bear solitude nor I a crowd. The quick coupled with the dead.

TRELAWNY

She has considerable character, but of a somewhat dispirited nature.

SHELLEY

What Mary is when she smiles, I can no longer tell or call to mind. It's a miracle so rare. We make a despairingly disparate couple today. But let events follow their natural course. I am not like the other apes of humanity who make mouths in the glass of the time. Mary and I live like crabs, each to his own shell. I have even been advised to divide my house. Give Mary the outside and keep the inside for myself.

TRELAWNY

I suspect that Miss Claironsti's absence must weigh heavily on you both, now that she has removed to Florence. I miss her company particularly.

SHELLEY

So we had noticed. Well, Claire may have deserted us, but we still have Jane. What else remains to me? Domestic peace and fame? You will laugh when you hear me talk of the latter. Domestic peace I might have, but have not, for Mary suffers dreadfully from the state of her father's circumstances.

Godwin is a vulture. Vultures, as you know, have considerable appetites.

TRELAWNY

I had supposed that a person of such renown in the publishing world would have few impediments to a peaceful old age.

SHELLEY

Renown? The only renown Godwin ever had was to be the husband of Mary's mother. For thirty years he has lived off the notoriety of *The Rights of Women,* a book of some consequence. It has greatly influenced Mary's philosophy.

TRELAWNY

Mrs Wollstonecraft too was against marriage, was she not?

SHELLEY

She claimed that marriage would never be held sacred until women were prepared to be their husband's companions rather than their mistresses. Mary and I have always striven to remain companions, but I wish she were as wise now as she will be at forty-five. She would then live on very good terms with Claire.

TRELAWNY

A complicated but fascinating young woman. The night before she left us, I woke to hear someone creeping past my door. On opening it a crack I spied Miss Clairmont carrying a candle along the passage. Rather like Lady Macbeth.

SHELLEY

Did you indeed? I expect the chimney board in Claire's room was found to have walked into the middle of the landing again accompanied by the pillow. Being very sleepy, it tried to get back into bed but fell down on its back. Claire has suffered from insomnia since Allegra's death. She is the subject of my only novel, damned by public opinion as fit only for the inmates of a brothel. Perhaps because of its association with Claire, I still have a deep affection for that work. Authors, like mothers prefer the children who have given them the most trouble.

SCENE NINE: SHELLEY/EDWARD/ TRELAWNY/MARY/JANE

MARY, JANE and EDWARD enter, having finished dinner. MARY carries a tray with Trelawney's food on it. JANE carries a collection of art objects she bought recently from a traveling pedlar- a small statuette of a naked boy, a painting of Apollo and another of an old peasant woman.

MARY

I have brought your dinner up, Trelawny. We despaired of ever seeing you again.

TRELAWNY

You are too kind, Mrs Shelley. You need not have taken the trouble, really.

SHELLEY

(who has pounced on the statuette)

Look at those fig leaves, curse them! Why is a round tin thing more decent than a cylindrical marble one? Where did you find it?

JANE

We passed an itinerant pedlar this afternoon during our walk.

SHELLEY

(studying the portrait of an old peasant woman)

What an exceedingly ugly face! I should be a long time before I should make love to her. This *Apollo* now has a softness and a womanish vivacity – a boyish inexperience exceedingly delightful.

JANE

(handing Shelley a folded paper)

I found this in the packet of poems you gave me. It was written ten years ago. You must have mislaid it.

MARY

(taking the poem before Shelley can reach it)

Ten years ago you were still with Harriet. *She reads.* "Harriet! Let death all mortal ties dissolve, but ours shall not be mortal!" A poor prophesy indeed! Unhappy Harriet!

SHELLEY

I do not know that I have anything to reproach in my conduct and certainly nothing in my feelings and intentions towards the dead.

EDWARD

She drowned herself, I believe.

SHELLEY

Everyone does me full justice and bears testimony to the uprightness and liberality of my conduct to Harriet. There is a united voice in condemnation of the detestable Westbrooks.

MARY

Percy never had any strong attachment for Harriet. He was married to her when quite a boy, under circumstances so peculiar as could never have happened to anyone of so very strange a turn of mind as himself.

SHELLEY

While residing in obscure lodgings, I fell so dangerously ill as to feel the near approach of death. Having been most tenderly and carefully nursed by Harriet, a very young woman of little or no pretensions, the only way to reward her disinterested conduct seemed to marry her on my death bed, as I thought. As my widow, she would certainly have been provided for by my family. I, however, unexpectedly recovered.

MARY

It seems that poor Harriet, the most innocent of her abhorred and unnatural family, was driven from her father's house and descended the steps of prostitution until she finally lived with a groom of the name of Smith. When he deserted her, she killed herself.

SHELLEY

There can be no question that the beastly viper, her sister, unable to gain profit from her connection with me, secured to herself the Westbrook inheritance. Everything tends to prove that beyond the mere shock of so hideous a catastrophe having fallen on a human being once so closely connected to me, there would in any case have been little left to regret. For months afterward, however, I would take a glass of ale every night to help deaden my feelings.

MARY

We have since learnt from my father that he has evidence Harriet was unfaithful to Percy four months before we left England.

SHELLEY

Her lover at the time was apparently a captain in the Indian Army who was ordered abroad. When still a child Harriet admired the Red Coats. She thought the military the best as well as the most fascinating men in the world, though she used to declare she would never marry one. If she married anyone it should be a clergyman.

MARY

You may conceive with what horror she first heard that Percy was an atheist.

SHELLEY

At first she did not comprehend the word. When it was explained to her, she was truly petrified. She wondered how I could live a moment professing such principles. She solemnly declared she would never change hers. When she wrote to me, she used to try and shake my principles, making sure that I was in the wrong and that she was right. She believed in eternal punishment and was dreadfully afraid of the Devil. She often dreamed of him and felt great terror whenever his name was mentioned.

MARY

Poor sad Harriet!

EDWARD

Suicide is a sin. Perhaps she has made the Devil's acquaintance. What do you think, Shelley?

SHELLEY

I think I should have liked to be a sailor. Tre says I cannot.

JANE

Why not?

TRELAWNY

Because he cannot smoke or drink or swear and these are essential qualifications for a sailor. You will do no good with him until you heave his books and papers overboard, shear the wisps of hair that hang over his eyes and plunge his arms up to the elbows in a tar bucket. Then he can't swim, which does not improve the situation.

SHELLEY

Why can't I swim? It seems so easy.

TRELAWNY

Because you think you can't. If you determine to do it, you will. All my efforts to teach our poet to swim have failed. I explained how to float, so he jumped in and lay stretched out on the bottom like a conger eel, not making the least effort to save himself.

SHELLEY

I always find the bottom of a well, remember. They say the truth lies there. If you had left me another minute, I would have found it and you would have found an empty shell. It is an easy way of getting rid of the body.

TRELAWNY

What would Mrs. Shelley have said to me if I had come home with your empty shell?

SHELLEY

Don't tell Mary! Not a word! It was a great temptation. In another minute I might have been on another planet.

TRELAWNY

But as you always find the bottom, you might have sunk deeper than did ever plummet sound.

SHELLEY

I am quite easy on that subject. Death is but the veil which those who live call life. They sleep and it is lifted.

JANE

That is far too nebulous for me.

MARY

Percy is nebulous. In the evening he goes out to take a little walk and loses himself half a mile from the villa. I am always afraid he will meet some villain skulking in the woods with a pistol.

TRELAWNY

Have no fear, Mrs Shelley. Your husband is very handy with a pistol, brandishing his weapon to scare away a gang of peasants. I do not call that particularly nebulous.

MARY

Even *Prometheus Unbound* has an insubstantial quality.

SHELLEY

Prometheus was written chiefly upon the mountainous ruins of the Baths of Caracalla, among flowery glades and thickets of blossoming trees. They extend in ever winding labyrinths upon immense platforms and dizzy arches, suspended in the air. The bright blue sky of Rome and the effects of the vigorous awakening spring were the inspiration of this drama. Prometheus is the type of highest perfection of a moral and intellectual nature. He is driven by the purest and truest motives to the best and noblest ends. It is a poem in my best style, the most perfect of my productions, the best thing I ever wrote, my favorite work.

EDWARD

Your mentioning Rome reminds me that we have just received a very late letter from Severn, announcing Keats' death. Shall I read it? "Poor Keats is dead. He died with the most perfect ease. He seemed to go to sleep. On the 23rd at half past four the approaches of death came on. "S lift me up, for I am dying," he murmured. "I shall die easy. Don't be frightened. Thank God it has come." I lifted him in my arms. The phlegm seemed to boil in his throat. This increased until 11 at night when he gradually sank into death, so quietly that I thought he slept."

By the beginning of 1820 the evidence of Keats' tuberculosis was clear. On hearing of his condition, Shelley wrote, offering him hospitality at Pisa, but Keats did not accept. Joseph Severn agreed to accompany him to Rome, where he died on February 23rd, 1821.

SHELLEY

Dead in Rome and under such lamentable circumstances! All lovers of poetry may regret him as a young genius destined to great things.

TRELAWNY

Last night I nearly put an end to our poet and myself. The wind was blowing very hard and fair. We returned late against a high sea and heavy wind. The boat behaved excellently, but we started with a huge sail and at ten o'clock capsized her.

SHELLEY

The ducking only added fire instead of quenching the nautical ardor which produced it. Both Williams and Tre declare the *Don Juan* to be perfect. I participate in their enthusiasm, in as much as would be decent in a landsman. We have been out again today and sought in vain for an opportunity of trying her against the feluccas or other larger craft in the bay. She passes the small ones like a comet might pass the dullest planet in heaven. She is swift and beautiful. We drive along the delightful bay in the off-shore breeze until the earth appears another world.

TRELAWNY

Another world indeed! If we had struck a squall today with the main-sheet jammed and the tiller put starboard instead of port, we should have had to swim for it.

SHELLEY

Not I. I should have gone down with the rest of the pigs in the bottom of the boat.

EDWARD

You will admit she fetches whatever she looks at. We now have a perfect plaything for the summer.

SHELLEY

At once a study and a carriage!

MARY

I do not understand why you need to change the mast for a bigger one, if the *Don Juan* is so perfect.

SHELLEY

To beat the feluccas, dear girl. To beat the feluccas!

JANE

Why is she named after Lord Byron's epic poem? You might have called her *Prometheus* or *Hellas*.

SHELLEY

Lord B arranged with Roberts for her construction along with his own new schooner. He never consulted us beforehand. We must suppose the name to have been given her during some equivocation of sex which her godfather suffered in his harem.

Captain Daniel Roberts, a retired Royal Naval Commander and friend of Trelawny, built both Byron's schooner 'Bolivar' and Shelley's smaller boat 'Don Juan'. It was based on a model Williams had brought from England, a plan Trelawny said Williams insisted upon against Robert's advice.

EDWARD

A surprising liberty to take. Did you not contest the name?

SHELLEY

I have lived too long near Lord Byron. The sun has extinguished the glow worm. I have ceased to appeal to his sense of decency and despair of rivaling him, as well I may. In any case, there is no other with whom it is worth contending.

JANE

Have you always aspired to be a poet?

SHELLEY

Classical reading and poetical writing occupied me already during my truncated residence at Oxford. At the same time, I became, in the popular sense of the word, an atheist. I printed a pamphlet avowing my opinion and distributed it to men of thought and learning. I believed that reason alone should decide on the issue. It was never my intention to deny it. Mr. Coplestone showed it to the masters and fellows of University College. I was sent for suddenly and went to the common room. There I found our master and two or three of the fellows. The master produced a copy of the pamphlet and asked me if I were the author. He informed me that if I denied the publication no more would be said. He spoke in a rude, abrupt and insolent tone. I begged to be informed for what purpose he put the question. No answer was given. "If I can judge from your manner," I said, "you are resolved to punish me, if I should acknowledge that it is my work. If you can prove it is, produce your evidence. It is neither just nor lawful to interrogate me in such a case for such a purpose. Such proceeding would better suit a court of the Spanish Inquisition. I did write the work and see nothing in it of which I have not reason to be proud." And so I was expelled.

EDWARD

So we learnt from the Gisbornes. Incidentally, your Italian manservant and his wife have found favor and a situation with them.

MARY

We had to get rid of Paolo. He cheated us through thick and thin of £1,000. We discovered that our maid, Elise, had formed an attachment with Paolo when we proceeded from Este to Rome and at Naples their marriage was talked of.

SHELLEY

We all tried to dissuade her.

MARY

We knew Paolo to be a rascal and we thought so well of Elise that we believed him to be unworthy of her.

SHELLEY

An accident led Mary to the knowledge that, without marrying, they had formed a connection. So we sent for a doctor who said there was danger of a miscarriage.

MARY

We could not turn the girl out on the world without in some degree binding her to this man.

SHELLEY

So we had them married at the British Counsel. Elise left us, turned Catholic and they went to live in Florence, where she suffered a miscarriage, a distressing experience to which Mary is no stranger. The last time it occurred, we were in an extremely isolated spot. Mary's condition for some hours was most alarming. With no medical assistance to hand I had to take the most decisive resolutions.

MARY

He made me sit in ice and succeeded in checking the hemorrhage and the fainting fits. When the physician finally arrived, all danger was over. He had nothing to do but to applaud Percy for his boldness.

SHELLEY leaps to his feet, shielding his eyes, as if from a dazzling light.

SHELLEY

There it is again! There! A naked child rising from the sea foam. See how joyfully she claps her hands. Now she will raise her hands to reveal....See? It is my own face, asking the same question, always the same question: "Shelley, siete sodddisfato? Siete soddisfato?"

For a few seconds he leans against the wall, his eyes open, but evidently unconscious, repeating the words. Then with a sudden gasp he stumbles onto the terrace and vanishes.

JANE

Good God! Can he have leapt from the wall? Where can he be gone?

With a gesture of irritation and yet worried preoccupation, MARY hurries after him.

Scene Ten: Jane/Edward/Trelawny

JANE

What an extraordinary man! Have you remarked how he often presents past events as they might have been, not as they really were?

EDWARD

You do not believe his stories about Oxford or his first marriage?

JANE

I am convinced that he is incapable of giving an account according to the strict truth or the bare realities of actual life. His reactions are most unpredictable.

TRELAWNY

On the occasion of our very first meeting, I told him I had once met his sister. After giving me a cold stare, he walked out of the room without a word.

JANE

He greatly suffers from the loss of his sister's affection. A man who lives so totally out of the ordinary world of ideas needs an ever-present sympathy more than the general run of men.

TRELAWNY

Which is hardly the case with Lord B. Byron likes and is satisfied to corrupt a girl's mind without necessarily seducing her at first. He likes to dawdle over her bosom, to inhale her breath, to lean against her thigh and play with the hem of her petticoats. Rather than make the effort of relieving his mind by furious gratification, he keeps his feelings tingling by imagining the rest. Nevertheless, Byron is as perfect a gentleman as ever crossed a drawing-room, when he likes and where he likes.

EDWARD

Surely there can be no radical distinction between the private and public character of a poet? If a poet sympathizes and justifies wickedness in his poetry, he is a wicked man. It hardly matters that his private life may be free from wicked actions.

JANE

That is hardly the case with Lord B.

TRELAWNY

Oh, Byron does have a conscience, although the world gives him no credit for it. He is now repenting, not of the few sins he has committed, but of the many he has not committed.

EDWARD

Byron thinks Shelley by far the most imaginative poet of the day. If he only wrote as he talked, he would be popular enough. Shelley takes criticism too much to heart although he denies this most vehemently.

TRELAWNY

When Byron is attacked by a critic, instead of bursting a blood vessel, he drinks three bottles of claret. It is a mystery how he manages to produce such wonderfully lucid ideas. In his household all is confusion. The cut-throats he is so desirous to have about him have involved him in numerous rows. His reception of Mrs Hunt last month was most shameful. She came into his house sick and exhausted and he scarcely deigned to notice her He remained silent and never bowed. As to friendship, it is a propensity in which Byron's genius is very limited. He does not know a single human being, except Lord Clare, for whom he feels nothing that deserves the name. He does not even feel it for Shelley, however much he admires and esteems him.

JANE

Percy is too sentimental and tender for Lord B.

EDWARD

Perhaps a dram too eccentric also. His cousin Medwin told me once that in Leicester Square one morning at five o'clock he was attracted by a group of boys collected round a well-dressed person lying near the rails. It was Shelley. He had spent the night on the pavement and could give no account of how he got there.

TRELAWNY

An overdose of laudanum, I should imagine. Our poet is convinced that he suffers from a dozen different fatal diseases and is headed for a premature demise in a leper colony.

JANE

Nonetheless, mysterious. Almost as mysterious as their sudden flight from Naples. Apparently they were afraid of being arrested for a fraudulent birth registration. At the time the Shelleys were in Naples, Claire was with child again.

EDWARD

By Shelley surely. She had been forbidden access to Byron. You may remember she wrote you that she was constantly unwell and under the care of a physician.

JANE

We were charitable enough to believe that the quantity of medicine she then took was not for the mere purpose of restoring her health.

TRELAWNY

Miss Clairmont is a pretty but foolish girl. Byron could not exactly play the stoic with a woman who had scrambled eight hundred miles to unphilosophize him. By the by, what was all the rumpus last night? It woke me up.

EDWARD

Shelley saw spirits again and alarmed the whole house.

JANE

He burst out of their bedroom screaming. This inspired Mary with such a panic that she jumped out of bed and ran across the landing to our room, where she fell to the floor.

SHELLEY returns very much disturbed.

What's the matter, Percy?

SHELLEY

Mary has threatened me.

JANE

Threatened you with what? To box your ears?

SHELLEY

Oh, much worse than that. Mary insists that she will have a musical party. There is an English family in the region. They sing madrigals and Mary has invited them here. Oh, the horror! It will kill me.

JANE

Music kill you! Why, you told me, you flatterer, that you loved music.

SHELLEY

So I do. It's the company that terrifies me. For pity's sake go to Mary and intercede for me. I will submit to any species of torture than that of being bored to death by idle ladies and gentlemen.

EDWARD

Let Tre and I go, my dear, and use our masculine powers of persuasion.

They hurry out in search of Mary. SHELLEY flings himself on the sofa dramatically. JANE sits beside him and smooths his forehead.

Scene Eleven: Jane/Shelley

SHELLEY

My head is rather dizzy today on account of this appalling news, not taking enough rest and a slight attack of typhus.

JANE

Would you like me to play for you?

SHELLEY

That would be exceedingly delightful. *JANE takes her guitar and plays softly while SHELLEY continues to talk.* This afternoon I lay under the olives trees and had a strange vision. I stood upon the brink of a platform of cliff and watched the ever-moving water stream down. It fell in thick and tawny folds, flaking off the rock face. It did not seem hollow within, but without it was unequal like the folding of linen thrown carelessly down. My eyes followed it and it evaporated below in its own foam and spray, in the cloud-like vapors boiling up from below. Not like rain, nor mist, nor spray, but water in a shape unlike anything I ever saw before. On the shoreline below, beyond the lance-shaped olive leaves, the sea crept with little lapping wavelets over the gray stones. The wide main stretched away, checkered with sunbeams and shade, like a poetic thought, as evanescent as the wrinkled sand over which the waves wash.

JANE

You make such observations so sorrowful.

SHELLEY

My sorrows are not so undeserved as you seem to believe. Elizabeth would have understood. She was a great consolation to me, but she is gone, lost to me forever. Married to a clod of earth, she has become as insensitive herself. All those fine capabilities mouldered!

JANE

You speak of your sister as a lover might.

SHELLEY

Like many other incorrect things, incest is a very poetical circumstance. All poets have an incestuous vein coursing through their bodies. Lord B is a perfect example. A person of consummate genius, he is capable, if he would direct his energies to such an end, of becoming the redeemer of his degraded country. It is his weakness to be proud. From a comparison of his own extraordinary mind with the dwarfish intellects that surround him he derives an intense apprehension of the nothingness of life. His passions and his powers are incomparably greater than those of most men, but he is unable to use them, for his ambition preys upon itself. It is on his own hopes and affections only that he seems to trample. Lord Byron is an exceedingly interesting person. Is it not to be regretted that he is a slave to the vilest and most vulgar prejudices and as mad as the winds? I see reason to regret this union of great genius and the things which make great genius useless.

JANE

His treatment of Claire must have greatly upset both you and Mary.

SHELLEY

Many circumstances have occurred between myself and Lord B which make intercourse painful. Our last discussion about money particularly so. Between ourselves, I greatly fear the alliance with Lord B will not succeed much longer. I can not consent to be no more than the link of the two thunderbolts.

JANE

But are not your aims similar?

SHELLEY

I cannot vouch for Albé. My aim has always been to break through the crust of outworn opinions. Established institutions depend on them. I appeal to the most universal of all feelings: Love. Unfortunately there is an incompatibility between love and creation. I have lost my life, first to Life, then to Death. Neither is the love I seek and both have deceived me. I have intrenched myself like a spider in a web.

JANE

How depressing! Tell me, Percy, what do you really mean when you say you love somebody? Surely you mean, as Edward thinks, that you merely possess them, or desire to possess them.

SHELLEY

The love I mean is celebrated everywhere as the sole law which should govern the moral world. My language is misunderstood as usual. I describe love as that powerful attraction towards all that we conceive or fear or hope beyond ourselves.

JANE

The love that passeth all understanding? I thought you were an atheist?

SHELLEY

Because we do not love and because we are not happy, we invest in God, thinking He will bring us happiness. You cannot love if your object is merely to achieve a result.

JANE

Poor God! Only an investment. Little wonder the Church disapproves of your writings.

SHELLEY

If I have attacked religion, it is agreed that I am punishable, but not by the loss of my children. When I think of what I have endured of enmity and contempt from all mankind. Prejudices are so violent and in contradiction to my principles. More people hate me as a freethinker than love me as a votary of freedom. Hatred and resentment are very disturbing qualities. The life of a man of virtue and talent, who should die in his thirtieth year is, with regard to his own feelings, longer than that of a miserable priest-ridden slave who dreams out a century of dullness. The great instrument of moral good is the imagination. It administers to the effect by acting upon the cause. If it were possible that a person should give a faithful account of his being from the earliest minutes of his recollections, a picture would be presented, such as the world has never contemplated before. A mirror would be held up to all men in which they might behold their own recollections. In dim perspective they would see their shadowy hopes and fears, all they dare not, or that daring and desiring, they could not expose to the open light of day.

JANE

We all have hopes and fears. That is part of human nature. Had you no hopes when you first met Mary or Harriet before her?

SHELLEY

All women are but the mortal manifestation of the unknown nameless muse. It has haunted me nightly since as far back as I can recall. In my boyhood dreams she pressed kisses upon my lips. From a terrible solitude I contemplated love like a wretched but content prisoner. I awoke every night from dreams that denied delicious desire. She held me in her arms. I nearly died of madness and delight. But she was only the vision of a delirious and distempered dream. She had no more color than an autumn sunset. Who is there that will not pursue phantoms? We spend our choicest hours in hunting after dreams and then wake only to perceive our error and regret that death is so near. Now I am haunted by the ghosts of old remembrances. They all contrive to make me some reproach to which there is no reply.

JANE

Perhaps you could not have prevented Harriet's desperate act after all. Perhaps she loved a being, an idea in her own mind which had no real existence. She concreted this abstract perfection. She annexed this fictitious quality to the idea presented by a name.

SHELLEY

The being whom the name signified, however, was by no means worthy of such worship.

JANE

She was very young. Only sixteen.

SHELLEY

Her knowledge was very confined on account of her youth. When she lived with her father, she was not likely to gain much. Their circle of acquaintance was very limited. Her father did not think it proper that they should mix much with society. After we had exchanged vows of eternal love, her school fellows would not speak to her and would not even reply to her questions. They called her an abandoned wretch and universally hated her. She often discoursed of her purpose of killing herself one day. Well, that is all very fine and nothing new. The world has heard so much and people may believe or not believe, as they think good. On a more positive note, you may have noticed that Mary begins for the first time to look a little consoled. We have spent, as you may imagine, a miserable twelve months since the deaths of Clara and William. You may not be aware, but Mary has great fortitude. I have suffered much to find out and have always considered her much my superior.

MARY enters waving a letter just received.

MARY

Lady Cashell writes that the very interesting Italian lady we met last winter in her house , I forget her name, Spremuta or something, is now married.

SHELLEY

Which, to quote our friend Peacock, is, you know, the same thing as being dead.

EDWARD enters dressed to go sailing.

EDWARD

Do make haste and prepare yourself, Shelley. If we are to reach Leghorn before sunset, we should weigh anchor immediately, while the breeze is holding.

MARY

Must you go, Percy? I beg you to stay until tomorrow and see if the weather is more settled. The air is so heavy and oppressive. I am sure it will burst upon us before long.

SHELLEY

Dear girl, we have made the trip a dozen times. In seven hours we shall be in Leghorn and send you word of our safe arrival.

MARY hangs round his neck, as if hoping to retain him by force. With a final kiss he frees himself and follows EDWARD out.

Scene Twelve: Mary/Jane

There is a long silence. Both women look fearfully after their husbands. MARY dabs her eyes with a handkerchief and sighs deeply. They exchange apprehensive looks as a distant roll of thunder troubles the silence.

MARY

Seven years are now gone since we left England. What changes! What a life! We now appear tranquil, but who knows what wind may yet blow? I will not prognosticate evil. We have had enough of it. When I came to Italy, I said all is well, if it were permanent. It has been more passing than an Italian twilight, but I still say the same. Yet that too has an end.

She wanders out onto the terrace and gazes out over the bay, where Shelley, Edward and a sailor are preparing the Don Juan for departure.

The thunderstorms that visit us here are grander and more terrific than I have ever seen before. One night we witnessed the finest storm. The whole bay was lit up, the pines on the headland made visible and all the scene illuminated for an instant. Then a pitchy blackness succeeded and the thunder came in frightful bursts over our heads amid the darkness.

JANE

As frightful as the lightning that accompanied the birth of your monstrous creation? *Frankenstein* is a wonderful work for a girl not nineteen at the time.

MARY

Shelley concedes that I have some dramatic talent. He is always most earnest and energetic in his exhortations that I should cultivate to the utmost any talent I possess. I must confess I still have an affection for my hideous progeny, for it was the offspring of happier days. Death and grief were only words then. They found no true echo in my heart. These pages speak of many a walk, many a drive and many a conversation when I was not alone.

JANE

Surely it has not always been thus?

MARY

Ten miles from Como is a villa called the Pliniana. Two large halls hung with splendid tapestry and paved with marble open on each side of a court. One side overlooks the deep, dark lake. The other is bounded by a mountain from whose stony side gushes with roar and splash the celebrated fountain. If some kind spirit had whispered forgetfulness to us, I think we should have been very happy there.

JANE

You still have your poet.

MARY

No, that time is past. I know it. If I can say anything about myself today, it will only be a list of hours spent in tears. My walks in the woods only make me weep and shudder. My only moments of peace are on board that unhappy boat out there. Lying down with my head on my knees, I shut my eyes and feel the wind and our swift motion alone. The movement mesmerizes me into the reassuring world of forgetfulness. For a few blessed minutes I can forget the loss of my two beloved children.

JANE

The premature death of our children is one of the curses of all womanhood.

MARY

After William's death I was silent to all around me. I hardly replied to the slightest question and was uneasy when I saw a human creature near me. I did not listen to their conversations. They seemed to me to be spoken in an unknown tongue. I found that if sorrow was dead within me, so was love and desire of sympathy. The living were not fit companions for me and I was constantly meditating by what means I might shake them off and never be heard of again. I became unfit for any intercourse. Captious and unreasonable, my temper was utterly spoilt. Everything on earth lost its interest to me. I was not fit for anything and therefore not fit to live. I was no stranger to human suffering. I had seen it on our long journey across France to Switzerland. The distress of the inhabitants gave a sting to my detestation of war. None who have not traveled through a country pillaged and wasted by this plague can feel what man in his pride inflicts upon his fellows. But let us not talk of those months. When I look back on all I have suffered, I shudder with horror. A sickening feeling steps in the way of every enjoyment when I think of it.

JANE

Trelawney believes that you three girls were all in love with Shelley and that Fanny put an end to her existence owing to his preference for the youngest sister.

MARY

What an extraordinary notion! Poor Fanny had long determined the best thing she could do was to put an end to her existence. Her birth was unfortunate and her life only a series of pain to those persons who had hurt their health in endeavoring to promote her welfare. Naturally to hear of her death gave us pain, but..

JANE

You soon had the blessing of forgetting that such a creature had ever existed.

MARY

We had the same mother, but were so different in character that it limited unfeigned intimacy to the point that we rarely communicated.

JANE

Fanny's father was an American painter, was he not?

MARY

He would have done better if he had limited his manifestations of affection to painting her portrait. I never saw Allegra without thinking of the expressions in my mother's letters concerning Imlay and their daughter. Claire's relationship with Lord B was very similar. She too was abandoned by the father of her child. After her first burst of grief and despair at Allegra's death, Claire reconciled herself to her fate much sooner than we expected. Byron's is a powerful mind, one that fills me with melancholy mixed with pleasure. It is always the case when intellectual energy is displayed. I remember so well our excursions on the lake at Geneva, how we saw him when he came down to welcome our arrival with a good-humored smile. How very vividly each line of his poetry recalls some scene of this kind to my memory.

JANE

Shelley is quite a different person from Byron, is he not? So gentle, so affectionate, so generous. He would not hurt a fly, I am sure.

MARY

Percy would save anything that had life. His integrity and sweetness of disposition are unequaled by any human being that ever existed, but he has never really liked society in numbers. Neither does he like loneliness. Usually he shelters himself against memory and reflection in a book or in the wildest regions of his fancy, in the air, under a tree, on the bank of a river. Somewhere an undivided spirit reigns, a mutual harmony among the works of nature.

JANE

Hunt considers S as the discoverer of the path to a pure and original spring of truth.

MARY

For the discovery of truth there is no path. A crowded mind, filled with facts and knowledge like Percy's, acts as an impediment to understanding anything as timeless as truth. Now he has a new plan, to go to Greece, when our heroic Mavrocordato has freed it from the Turks, to one of those beautiful islands where earth, ocean and sky form a paradise.

JANE

How very adventurous of you, my dear!

MARY

Not I! I am sure he has already inveigled Claire. He may go to Greece with her, if he chooses. I no longer have a taste for adventure. It died when baby Clara did. After her death my father asked me to bear in mind that it is only persons of a very ordinary sort that sink long under calamity. He assured me that such a recollection would be of great use to me. In his opinion we seldom indulge long in depression and mourning, except when we think secretly that there is something very refined in it or that it does us honor. I have become a very ordinary sort, shackled eternally to depression and mourning.

JANE

How does that affect your relationship with your father?

MARY

We have not met for seven years. Our correspondence is sporadic and mostly concerns his demands for more money to salvage his bookshop. It was never an easy affinity. My father seldom caressed me. If ever he stroked my head, or took me on his knee, I felt a mingled alarm and delight difficult to describe. Yet strange to say, my father loved me almost to idolatry. I knew this and repaid his affection with enthusiastic fondness, despite his reserve and my awe. He was something great and wiser and better than any other being. I was the sole creature he loved, the object of all his thoughts by day and his dreams by night. When a father is all that a father may be, the love of a daughter is one of the deepest and strongest, the purest passion of which our natures are capable.

JANE

You never knew your mother, which naturally deepens the bond you feel for your father.

MARY

I never knew my dear mother, but she left me a part of herself. On her deathbed she wrote her last letter to me, the baby whose birth had killed her. I carry it with me everywhere, even though I learnt it by heart many years ago. "Death may snatch me from you before you can weigh my advice or enter into my reasoning. I would then with fond anxiety lead you very early in life to form your grand principle of action and save you from the vain regret of having, through irresolution, let the spring-tide of existence pass away, unimproved, unenjoyed. Gain experience – ah! Gain it, while experience is worth having and acquire sufficient fortitude to pursue your own happiness."

JANE

She must have been a remarkable woman. You have inherited her outstanding stature.

MARY

I inherited many things from her, among others depression and a tendency to introversion. As a girl I was not confined to my own identity. I could people the hours with creations far more interesting to me at that age than my own sensations. Like my mother, I am reputed to be a singularly bold, somewhat imperious young woman. Percy can vouch for that. He accuses me of constantly giving orders and treating him like a dog. Maybe I have good cause. There is little trust between us. He writes verses to Claire which he hides from me.

JANE

Only for fear of wounding you, I am certain.

MARY

Despite everything I sincerely wish him to acquire popularity. I believe that he will obtain a greater mastery of his own powers and greater happiness in his own mind if public applause crowns his endeavors.

JANE

What are your thoughts on our buccaneering guest?

MARY

Trelawney is a man who like seaweed, when in its element, unfolds itself and becomes a plant of rare beauty and grace. Taken from its element it is a worthless and ugly weed, trodden underfoot without remorse. Yet that same weed, if you raise it from the ground and tend on it, dividing and nursing its delicate forms will preserve its beauty. I do not despair of him.

JANE

He has heard from Lord Byron, who received letters from your servant Paolo claiming that both you and Claire share Shelley's bed.

MARY

Paolo is a most superlative rascal. I am glad we have done with him. You know Shelley and can you believe such false accusations on the testimony of a man we despise? I had hopes that such a thing was impossible and that although strangers may believe such calumnies, no one who has ever seen my husband can for a moment credit them. Paolo claims that Claire is Shelley's mistress, that … upon my soul, I solemnly swear I cannot say the words. I had rather die than repeat anything so vilely, so wickedly false and fiendish beyond all imagination. I am perfectly convinced in my own mind that Shelley has never had an improper connection with Claire. At the time specified by Elise and her husband, we lived in lodgings where I had entrance into every room. Such a thing could not have passed unknown to me. The union between my husband and myself has always been undisturbed. Though others sometimes see the worst part of my temper towards S, they have not seen the amends and requests of pardon I always make him in private.

TRELAWNEY enters, visibly irate.

TRELAWNEY

They have left, despite my pressing admonition to wait until tomorrow. Shelley would have stayed, but Williams urged him to relent. The anchor is weighed, the sail hoisted and the course set north west.

A louder roll of thunder rumbles from afar. Trelawney draws his spyglass from his pocket, hastens out onto the terrace and begins to scan the horizon. The thunder becomes more insistent, accompanied by a flash of lightning. MARY utters a scream and falls inert to the floor.

BLACKOUT

EPILOGUE

TRELAWNEY

(alone downstage in a spotlight)

They had left the bay at a little after twelve with a light and favorable breeze from the SE. At half past three the sun became overcast. Small dark clouds rising from the sea ascended and moved rapidly along against the wind, which indicated a change to the NW. The horizon in that quarter became dense and alarming. I climbed the castle tower and saw through my glass the *Don Juan* about ten miles out to sea. They were taking in their topsails. The haze of the storm, however, soon hid the boat. Twenty minutes later, after the storm had cleared, I looked again, fancying that I should see them returning, but there was now no boat on the sea.

On the morning of the third day I rode to Pisa and went upstairs to Byron. When I told him my fears, his lip quivered and his voice faltered. He dispatched the *Bolivar* to cruise along the coast. I mounted my horse and rode in the same direction. I stimulated the coast guard to keep a lookout by promise of a reward.

Many days later two bodies were found on the shore. The face and hands and parts of the body not protected by clothing were fleshless. The tall slight figure, the jacket, the volume of Sophocles in one pocket and Keat's poems in the other, doubled back, as if the reader had hastily thrust it away, were all too familiar to me to leave any doubt that this mutilated corpse was any other than Shelley's.

In view of the advanced state of decomposition it was decided to resort to the ancient Greek custom of burning and reducing the body to ashes. I got a furnace made at Leghorn, iron bars and strong sheet iron supported on a stand. I received a note from Byron to say he would join us on the beach as near noon as he could. The spot where the body lay buried was marked by the gnarled root of a pine tree. The soldiers set to work. Shoveling away the sand which covered the body, they soon uncovered the end of a black silk handkerchief, then some shreds of linen and a boot with the bone of the leg and the foot in it. All that now remained of the poet was a shapeless mass of bones and flesh which the soldiers moved piecemeal onto the stand. "Don't repeat this with me," said Byron, "let my carcass rot where it falls. The entrails of a worm hold together longer than the potter's clay of which man is made."

The funereal pyre was now ready. As soon as the flames allowed us to approach, we threw frankincense and salt into the fire and poured a flask of wine and oil over the burning remains. At four o'clock the pyre burnt low. Nothing remained but dark ashes and fragments of the larger bones.

Our Pisa circle is not one to be forgotten. There was no other such in the wide world, such hearts united under the sunny clime of Italy. Such scenes and events no time can fade.

Blackout. When the lights return MARY is seen sitting in the same position as in the beginning of the play.

MARY

I remember how hopelessly I have lingered on the Italian soil for five years, waiting for a favorable change. Instead of which, I am now leaving it, having buried here everything I loved. Was it all in vain? I see no mountains or valleys, woods or rushing streams. I see only my lost darling. Oh, my beloved Shelley, when spring arrives, leaves you never saw will shadow the ground, flowers you never beheld will star it. My own heart, I would fain know what you think of my desolate state, what you think I ought to do, what to think. It is not true that this heart was cold to you. Did I not in the deepest solitude of thought repeat to myself again and again my good fortune in possessing you?

CURTAIN

The ashes of PERCY BYSSHE SHELLEY were taken to Rome. He had expressed the wish to be buried in the same grave as little William, but when the grave was opened it was found to contain the remains of an unknown adult. The ashes found a final resting place in a solitary place below the ruins of a tall tower, part of the old Roman wall. Trelawny inscribed the gravestone with lines from The Tempest: *"Nothing of him that doth fade, but doth suffer a sea-change into something rich and strange."*

After her husband's death, MARY SHELLEY returned to England and devoted the rest of her life to educating her only surviving child, Percy Florence. Shelley's father, Sir Timothy, made only a small allowance for his grandson's education and when, in 1844, Sir Timothy died at the age of 90, she was by that time too ill to derive much pleasure from her relative affluence. In 1851 she died in London, 29 years after her husband.

JANE WILLIAMS returned to England before Mary, who had given her a letter of introduction to Jefferson Hogg, her husband's best friend from the Oxford days. Jane and Hogg soon became lovers and had two children. She died in 1862.

With financial help from Trelawney and Mary, CLAIRE CLAIRMONT went to Moscow as governess in a prosperous family. Ten years later she was still talking of her continuing love of Shelley. She made her home for the last twenty years of her life in Florence, having come into the £12,000 legacy Shelley left her when Sir Timothy died.

EDWARD TRELAWNEY accompanied Byron to the Greek War of Independence, where Byron died of malaria the following year. He traveled extensively and enjoyed being lionized by London society. He retired to Sussex, where he died in 1881. His ashes were buried in the grave he had reserved next to Shelley's in Rome 60 years earlier.

Lightning Source UK Ltd.
Milton Keynes UK
UKOW041211030713

213127UK00001B/12/P